THE HIDDEN TREASURE IN YOUR WEBSITE

The First Professional Guide to Monetizing Your Website with In-Text Advertising

Tomer Treves

iUniverse, Inc.
Bloomington

The Hidden Treasure in Your Website
The First Professional Guide to Monetizing Your Website with In-Text Advertising

iUniverse books may be ordered through booksellers or by contacting:

iUniverse
1663 Liberty Drive
Bloomington, IN 47403
www.iuniverse.com
1-800-Authors (1-800-288-4677)

Because of the dynamic nature of the Internet, any Web addresses or links contained in this book may have changed since publication and may no longer be valid. The views expressed in this work are solely those of the author and do not necessarily reflect the views of the publisher, and the publisher hereby disclaims any responsibility for them.

Any people depicted in stock imagery provided by Thinkstock are models, and such images are being used for illustrative purposes only.

Certain stock imagery © Thinkstock.

ISBN: 978-1-4502-8899-6 (pbk)
ISBN: 978-1-4502-8901-6 (cloth)
ISBN: 978-1-4502-8900-9 (ebk)

Library of Congress Control Number: 2011902450

Printed in the United States of America

iUniverse rev. date: 5/17/2011

Contents

Introduction   vii

Chapter 1: The Site Monetization Challenge and the In-Text Advertising Answer   1

Chapter 2: In-Text Advertising Explained—Terminology, Technology, Ideology   9

Chapter 3: Technology Basics of In-Text Advertising   19

Chapter 4: Advanced Website Monetization with In-Text Ads   23

Chapter 5: In-Text Advertising Networks and Providers   38

Chapter 6: In-Text Advertising Revenue and Earnings   43

Chapter 7: In-Text Advertising Extras   60

Chapter 8: Popular Questions   75

Chapter 9: Conclusions and the $1,000 Coupon   98

About the Author   103

Index   105

Introduction

The Internet was born free, has changed our way of life, and should stay pure and free of any capitalist interests, right? Well ... that's a romantic notion, but let's have a reality check. The Internet is a wonderful communication tool and a magnificent source of information, but *it is not free.* While people expect it to be free, any blogger or website publisher will tell you that his costs are very real. And in the real world, somebody needs to pay the bill. At a minimum, bloggers and website owners spend a lot of time on their websites, and no matter how much we pretend otherwise, time is money. Yet, most information on the Internet is given away for the attractive price of "zero." As a result, bloggers and publishers must find other ways to make money from their websites—first, to cover their costs, and second, to earn profit.

The most common method of website monetization is placing advertising on your website or blog and getting paid by advertisers who seek the attention of your site visitors. The problem is that these ads interfere with the user's experience. Even worse, they don't pay enough.

Recently, a new form of online advertising—in-text advertising— has begun to offer website publishers an additional source of revenue that is very easy to implement and doesn't take up space on your site. With in-text advertising, which is actually a new form of permission marketing, the advertisements are placed as hyperlinks within your existing text. In-text ads are mostly identified as double-underline links within the website's content. When your site visitor's mouse hovers over the area where the link is imbedded, a bubble with an advertisement opens.

This book is the first professional guide that covers all aspects of integrating in-text ads on your websites and blogs. It isn't a long book, and it isn't complicated. But after reading it, you'll have a new, guaranteed source of revenue as a blogger or website owner. That's *guaranteed* money. Not many books can offer you that, can they?

Here is an overview of some of what you will learn:

- Why you need ads on your website.
- The advantages of in-text ads.
- The basic definitions and all required technological aspects of implementing in-text ads.
- Advanced integration of in-text ads.
- Potential improvements that can increase your earnings from in-text ads.
- Tips regarding the appearance of the links, choosing the best color, etc.
- The best places to put in-text ads on your site and where they should be turned off.
- How to analyze your in-text ads' performance according to the browsers of your visitors.
- How to choose the best in-text ad network for you.
- How to determine how much revenue you should earn with your in-text ads and how to get paid.
- Information about in-text extras.
- Information about other formats of in-text ads that are a little different from the mainstream method.
- The interrelations of in-text ads and Google AdSense.
- How to apply in-text ads to big websites and content in languages other than English.
- Answers to potential objections to in-text ads, which will help you along the way to your first payment.

Although this book is meant for website publishers, the last part of the book also discusses advertising with in-text ads. This will not only help you as a potential advertiser, but it will also help you better understand your advertising partners.

Plus, there's a $1,000 coupon on the last page of the book, just before the index! This coupon is the fruit of a deal closed with Infolinks, one of the top in-text ad networks, which also happens to be my employer. If you follow the advice in this book to uncover the hidden treasure in your website by integrating in-text ads and use this coupon, Infolinks will double your first month's earnings up to $1,000. Not bad for a start!

I've been actively involved in business development and marketing for the past six years, most of it in the online world. In the last two years I was part of the small team who brought the Infolinks in-text Advertising Network to the world, heading the marketing and sales efforts. During this period, I worked with many online advertising networks and with numerous website publishers integrating in-text Ads into their platforms and offerings. I helped both networks and publishers increase their earnings from online advertising through the usage of in-text ads and learned from them tremendously about the different aspects of this unique advertising method. Infolinks has become one of the top three in-text ads networks in the world and the fastest growing among them. I'm happy to share this experience here.

After reading this book, I firmly believe you'll be convinced to give in-text ads a try.

CHAPTER 1:

THE SITE MONETIZATION CHALLENGE AND THE IN-TEXT ADVERTISING ANSWER

Why Put Ads On Your Website?
To Make the World a Better Place

I like to wake up in the morning with a smile, knowing that my work contributes to the positive side of the world's delicate balance—don't you? Well, as strange as it may sound, I feel like I'm doing just that when I monetize websites. When we find ways to cover the costs of websites and blogs, we help make more information readily available for everyone. Now isn't that a nice thought to wake up with each morning?

But the bottom line is that websites need to make money. There are three typical ways of making money from a website: (1) charge visitors for usage, (2) sell something to visitors, and (3) expose visitors to ads. From these three methods, only the third—placing online ads—keeps the information available for free to the world.

I know, I know. Exposure to ads involves indirect costs and blurs our delicate minds, but unless you're ready to move to Mars it's already part of everything we do—the Internet included.

So, when we place ads on a website, we pick up the bill for the website's cost, and by doing so we give our site visitors more free information and make the world a better place. Recently, however, revenue from ads has shrunk, and many people claim that they don't provide enough money to justify free websites. Is that true?

Out of Sight, Out of Site—
Why is Revenue from Online Ads Dropping?

After several happy years of sharp angle graphs with numbers that grew at an insane rate, the trend began to change. Theoretically, the positive growth should have kept going up, but the recent economic downturn caused a decrease in advertising budgets in general. Nevertheless, online advertising budgets are still out there. Advertisers are seeking measurable and direct ways to communicate with their potential customers, and online advertising is the leading choice.

So what's the problem? Online ads have "disappeared" from websites. Okay, not literally ... the ads are still technically there. But site visitors no longer notice them. Just as with other media formats, people's minds began to screen the ads out of their consciousness. And what did the online marketing industry do to regain the consumers' attention? It created ads that disturb visitors and fight with the website's content for their attention. Wonderful companies like Eyeblaster pushed the evolution of banners forward and, in fact, saved the monetizing business. Banners began jumping around, animated characters walked onto our screens, full-page ads covered sites entirely, and when moving the mouse away from the content, we mistakenly activated sound from banner ads. Even the relatively quiet Google AdSense ads are now mostly replaced by animated banners. It seems like all efforts to withdraw the visitors' attention away from the content and onto the advertising is now legitimate.

But ads can't win this battle over the minds of people. As readers, we learn how to focus our attention on what we're looking for. And since it's the content we're interested in, not the jumping ads around it, we've evolved into human filters, reading content without noticing the ads. The truth is that exaggerated-reach media annoys visitors who then look for alternative sources of information. Only a very few will choose to pay a subscription to avoid ads, and most will simply move on to another site. With growing concerns about too many ads, serious online publishers choose very carefully which types of ads they put on their sites. But then readers give quieter ads less attention, which brings the advertising revenue down.

In a survey I ran regarding online readers' acceptance of a certain type of ad, I discovered that more than 30 percent hadn't noticed the ads. In fact, the multiple-choice answer that was chosen most often was this: "What, there were ads on that page?" According to younger online dwellers, they automatically disregard the commercial frame that usually surrounds the content. In fact, they don't even see it anymore.

While this behavior has not diminished revenue from online ads entirely, it has certainly reduced it. This is why I believe it's absolutely necessary to turn our attention to the hidden treasure in our websites.

The Hidden Treasure In Your Website

The solution to the ad problem is right there in the middle of your website. The content of the website can serve as a layer for placing subtle in-text ads. When used correctly, in-text ads appear as double-underline links within the content of a website. They don't interfere with the flow of reading, and they don't fight for the reader's attention. Your site's visitors know that these links lead to ads, but they don't have to be distracted by them. When a link interests the reader, he or she can hover over it with the mouse. Then a bubble will appear with a relevant ad inside. If interested, the visitor can click on the ad and continue to the advertiser's landing page. If not interested, the visitor simply moves the mouse away and continues reading.

In-text advertising is a great way to monetize a website. In-text ads complete other types of advertising without affecting them. If the in-text ads are relevant, they enrich the content with information that visitors find helpful and interesting. Yes, they are still ads, and readers would prefer that they weren't there, but the fact is that these ads generate the revenue you need to keep your information free. And this is something that your site visitors appreciate. Compared to jumping banners, in-text ads are the least intrusive method of advertising. Yet they are also highly relevant and yield good conversion rates for advertisers. This means that the online publisher is well paid.

With website revenue dropping, in-text advertising could save the day. If you look around, you'll see more and more in-text ads on the websites you visit. That's because now, several years after it was introduced, in-text advertising pays very well and has become a legitimate method of both advertising and monetizing.

From Absence through Protest to Legitimacy— The Advertising Penetration Cycle

I generally dislike discussions about new media that start with ancient history and the development of the Internet in the previous century. We're beyond that. However, the fact is that there's much to learn from comparing the media of the past with the Internet's evolution. If there is one clear pattern that has repeated itself in all media—newspapers, radio, broadcast television, cable television, and now the Internet—it's the penetration of advertising.

We've seen it before. First, there is a medium where ads are not allowed. Then there are organizations that protest against the appearance of first ads. Then there is the understanding that advertising helps reduce the costs of media access to the general public. From absence through protest to legitimacy, advertising penetrates all media.

This pattern was the same when ads first appeared in newspapers, and then on TV, and then on the web, and whenever a new type of advertising appears, it goes through this same cycle. Instead of looking deep into history books, the best example can be found by flipping back just a few pages to the introduction of ads on the e-mail service from Google.

In its early days, Gmail was available by invitation only, and when the ads showed up, early adopters actually liked the idea of a free service financed by the exposure to ads. (Before that, except for Hotmail perhaps, we had to pay for most good e-mail services. Remember that?) When Gmail started to spread, the ads surrounding the e-mails became the target of privacy organizations and concerned citizens. "The new Big Brother is reading our personal correspondence!" they complained. A short few years later, however, these ads became the standard. The advertising within the e-mail service from Google has become legitimate, and millions of people and businesses use Gmail worldwide, enjoying a good free service that is sponsored by ads.

In-text advertising is no different from other forms of advertising, and it's going through the same cycle. At first, as a new and exciting method, it was the talk of the day. Online leaders looked into it, and online giants Google, Microsoft, and Yahoo all attempted to use the technology. Then, it was deemed intrusive. The same type of people who were once against ads on TV and Gmail found the new form of ads "too much" because the ads rode on portions of the website's content. During 2008 and early 2009, in-text ads began to become legitimate. From absence through protest to legitimacy, in-text advertising now penetrates more and more websites.

CNNMoney.com published a *Fortune* magazine article in February 2009 about in-text advertising that called it the "one bright spot in online advertising":

> "It's hard to imagine a news site like the *New York Times* (nytimes.com) signing on (to in-text ads) without some uproar from readers and staff. Then again, the newspaper recently decided to sell ads on its front page to attract more revenue. And that, too, was once unthinkable."

Many other top websites are already displaying in-text ads: Fox News, MSNBC, Squidoo, Britannica, iVillage, JPost, BookRags, and eHow. Not convinced yet? Here are some more: esnips, The Hollywood Gossip, Ask The Builder, Money Control, Answer Bag, and many others.

By now, I can roughly estimate that 100,000+ websites have tried in-text ads, including major websites with substantial traffic. This significant number means that most surfers have seen an in-text ad somewhere by now. It also means that in each vertical content category, at least a few sites have implemented in-text ads, sowing the seeds of legitimacy that spreads on quickly.

On the other hand, there are more than 150 million websites worldwide, so 100,000 is still only a fraction. Take this fact, add the legitimacy factor, multiply it by the crazy-fast growth rate, and you have the phenomenal potential of in-text advertising. I bet you that the Internet giants will join this party soon. In-text advertising is on the verge of showing up everywhere online.

Interruption Advertising vs. Permission Marketing

What makes those double-underline links so promising as a method of advertising? It's the crucial difference between interruption and permission. Although this concept still seems very fresh, the idea was presented by Seth Godin a decade ago in his marvelous book, *Permission Marketing*. If you still haven't read it, it's never too late.

Traditional advertisements—TV commercials, newspaper ads, telemarketing phone calls, and even online display banners—are based on pulling people away from what they're doing. Godin calls this "Interruption Marketing" and shows how it's much less efficient to continuously interrupt people. In fact, he says it no longer works. Instead of annoying people, marketers should offer their potential customers incentives to accept advertising voluntarily. Godin calls this "Permission Marketing," and by now, ten years later, it is widely accepted as the fundamental basis for successful marketing strategies.

When we add more and more display ads on a website, making them larger, animated, and jumpy, or covering the entire content with a full-page ad, we're only pushing the traditional interruption advertising that no longer works. Excessive-reach media ads perform poorly for the advertiser, and since they annoy the website's visitors, they are eventually bad news for the website publisher as well.

At first, in-text ads were also considered intrusive and disruptive. The double-underline links appear within the text and are very difficult to avoid. But the double-underline link is a subtle hint to the reader that there is paid-for content concerning the highlighted term. That's it. In-text ads are very delicate and don't consume the reader's time or fight with the actual text for the reader's attention. The bubble appears with advertising inside it *only* if the reader actively shows interest by intentionally hovering over the link with the mouse. Compared to an animated banner or any other form of advertising, it's the least intrusive type of ad available. This is permission advertising at its best, and it gets even better.

After the bubble appears, the reader views the advertising content and makes a choice: either make the bubble disappear by moving the mouse away or click on the ad to follow it to the advertiser's landing page. This choice is the second time that permission is granted for the advertising. So, in-text ads are a form of double permission marketing with only minimal interruption.

For the advertiser, who pays only for actual clicks, the visitors are only those who actively chose to be exposed to the advertiser's content. They gave permission twice to spend time with the advertiser, which is the best possible start for a business relationship. When advertising works well for the advertiser, the website publisher is also happy because the advertiser is willing to pay accordingly. The publisher is also able to limit the interruption to site visitors and improve the chances that they'll return.

As long as the hint for the advertising is clear and the ad only shows up for the interested reader, in-text advertising leans heavily toward the right side of the fight between interruption advertising and permission marketing. It could be very tempting, however, to modify in-text ads into formats that mislead potential readers to believe they aren't about to be exposed to an ad. For the short term, this can indeed increase click rates. But for the long term, this practice will move the ads to the other side of the delicate balance toward interruption rather than permission. There are better ways. To increase clicks, conversions, and revenue, the algorithm needs to be improved and the integration optimized. There is a lot to this, and I intend to share my experience with you in this book—if you give me your kind permission.

7

The Publisher's Point of View

When advertising agencies discovered the Internet, they gave the new medium's ads different names: digital advertising, online advertising, interactive advertising, etc. But whatever the name, the first references and discussions involving the new advertising arena always came from the advertiser's point of view, such as how the advertising budget could be allocated online. Only later did the publisher's point of view come into play, such as how and why websites should place ads. First, there were services like Google AdWords and Yahoo Sponsored Search (i.e., the advertiser solutions). Only later came services like Google AdSense and Yahoo Content Match—the publisher solutions.

With in-text advertising, it was the other way around. The technology was initially embraced as a strong tool to monetize content on top of display ads, so in this case the publisher's point of view preceded the advertiser's angle. The newly formed bubbles presented advertisements to viewers that were meant to be either responses to search queries or part of a contextual advertising display. Initially, no online advertising budgets were allocated for in-text ads. Publishers were the first to come on board because they were looking for monetizing solutions. Advertisers joined in later, wishing to target in-text ads separately, using creative content that was different from other ad formats.

I intend to follow the same path. First, I'll analyze in-text advertising as hidden treasure for website publishers—a great website monetization tool. Then only as a secondary subject, I will discuss in-text advertising as a solution for advertisers—a great advertising channel.

CHAPTER 2:

IN-TEXT ADVERTISING EXPLAINED— TERMINOLOGY, TECHNOLOGY, IDEOLOGY

What is in-text Advertising?

In-text advertising is a method of advertising where the advertisements are placed as hyperlinks within existing text. (See the Wikipedia definition at http://en.wikipedia.org/wiki/In-Text_advertising.)

This short definition encapsulates the whole concept in just a few words, but further clarification is required. There are many reasons to include hyperlinks with in-text online. In fact, that's the essence of the web. But in this case, commercial interests direct the selection of the links. The term "advertisements" is important. There are other types of in-text placements that only add content and links to related content. These methods are not advertising since they don't include the placement of ads that lead to advertising content. The definition also mentions "within existing text," which means that in-text advertising is separated from other types of contextual advertising. While contextual ads can relate to the text but appear next to the text (like Google AdSense), and paid-for content can lead to text which is, in fact, an advertisement, in-text ads are placed *inside* content which was created independently and separately from the advertising.

In-text or In-Line?

The market has spoken: in-text advertising is the chosen term. In its early days, however, it was also called in-line or inline advertising. This name is less accurate, and it simply didn't spread enough before "In-Text" was coined and adopted.

There is still a question about the hyphen. Just as we all send emails to one another, and have stopped using e-mail, I believe in-text will evolve into intext (or at least InText to begin with), mainly because it's quite difficult to read it without the hyphen—the mind looks for other words to follow the word "in." For now, capitalizing helps the reading process.

Captain Hooks

Once an existing text is subject to in-text advertising, it is scanned, analyzed, and hyperlinks are added within the text, highlighting specific words or sentences. Each of these highlights is called a "hook." Why? I think of hooks as anchors for the most relevant advertising that has the potential to give the reader the most valuable ads. Since the term "anchor" already had a different use (anchors represent an internal target location for a hyperlink), another marine term was adopted. A way to remember the term "hook" is to think of the links as ways to "lure" readers to advertisements, just like hooks lure fish.

The number of hooks per a certain volume of text is an important factor, and so is the length of each hook. But before we go there, let's talk about the fact that most hooks are formatted with a double-underline.

Double-Underline Links

The most common method of highlighting the links for in-text ads is with a <u>double-underline</u>. This simple design was not in use as a symbol anywhere else online, so it sent a clear message to website visitors that these are not "regular" links—they're special. At first, the underlines may have simply attracted attention and generated more ad clicks. But soon, they became acknowledged as an accepted symbol, clearly indicating that this link leads to an advertisement.

As I wrote under Interruption Advertising vs. Permission Marketing, it's important to let readers know that these hyperlinks are a form of advertising in order to achieve success for the ads and the overall website user experience. An informed reader is less interrupted by the double-underline links while reading and only chooses to check them out when he has genuine interest in the advertisement. This means that the visitor is giving active permission to be exposed to the advertiser's content, which is the best possible start for both sides. Single-underline, which is used for other types of hyperlinks, confuses readers. Although this can lead to a short-term increase in clicks, it will lead to longer term dissatisfaction of both the website's visitors and the advertisers.

The Mouse Hover

When your website visitor reads an article, recognizes a term with double-underline as an ad, and wants to know a little more, what can he do? He simply hovers with the mouse over the link—sometimes referred to as a "mouse-over"—and a bubble appears with an advertisement inside. He looks at the ad, and if he's interested, he clicks on it and is taken directly to the advertiser's landing page. If he is not interested, he moves the mouse away from the double-underline, and the bubble disappears.

This active hover is a demonstration of interest by the reader—a very important aspect of this type of advertising, where permission is stronger than interruption. All parties involved—the reader, the website's publisher, and the advertiser—should be happier with this method. Despite the potential exposure to the ad's content, the business model is usually based on clicks, so the advertiser doesn't pay the website's publisher for the hover but only when a site visitor clicks on the ad. I will discuss business models more later on.

A Bubble, Not a Pop-Up

In-text advertising uses informative little cartoon-like bubbles in which the ads are placed with relevance to the highlighted term. There are different types of technology to create the bubbles, but in all cases, a bubble is not a "pop-up." Why? Well, the bubbles are part of the existing web page, and they don't send the user to a different location. Also, another strong proof is that the all-mighty pop-up filters don't block bubbles. The most important differentiator is that they are user-generated through the mouse hover. When interest is gone, the user can easily make them disappear by moving the mouse away—no clicks required.

The Top 9 Reasons Not to Use in-text Ads

If you've read this far, you know that I like in-text ads as a website monetization solution that doesn't interrupt visitors, and that I even work for Infolinks. But I also know that some people out there are still against in-text advertising. So to help them out, I have come up with the Top 9 reasons *not* to use in-text ads. This way, when your in-text-loving friends brag about their great ads, you'll be armed with some reasons why *not* to use them.

1. They don't jump around.

We all just love flashy, animated banners that do anything technology allows them to do to interrupt our reading, especially the banners that expand to cover half the page, make creepy noises, and hide the shut-down "x" so that we can't find it. As a website publisher, why would you want to use ads that are subtle, nonintrusive, quiet, and don't disturb your visitors while they're reading your content? Tell any in-text lovers that you want the jumpy ads with a video character that walks all over your precious writing, not those cute little unobtrusive double-underline links.

The Hidden Treasure in Your Website

2. Too much money is corruptive.

Having too much money leads to the illusion of power and then to corruption. Who needs it? in-text ads are known for generating extra revenue from a website without affecting other sources of income. Having all this extra cash is a slippery slope en route to corruption. Just say "no" to in-text ads, and you'll also say "no" to doubling your revenue.

3. Web programmers are losing jobs.

These are rough times, and with the economic downturn web programmers and developers are losing jobs. Integrating in-text ads into a website is way too easy. It can take less than a minute to simply paste a line of code into the website, and that's it. They require no changes to the website, no new code, no programming or developing, no IT, and no QA. So what will all our web programmer colleagues and friends do? Avoiding in-text ads will help them keep their jobs.

4. They make affiliate programs look bad.

Affiliate programs rule. We work hard to cooperate with affiliate programs and promote links to their sales efforts. Good affiliate plans have conversion rates of about 1 percent, which means that for every one hundred clicks we get on our website, we get one affiliation fee payment. Those in-text ads are on a pay-per-click basis (PPC), so the website publisher gets paid for every click. *Every click.* This makes our favorite pay-per-acquisition and pay-per-lead affiliate programs look bad!

5. You have to create real content.

When you have nothing new to write about in your blog, when you can't find any nice videos or images to upload, or when your website is left empty of new content, where do you turn? Advertising banners! We cover our website with advertising real estate: big squares, skyscrapers, leaderboards, whatever we can get our hands on to fill all of that space. Who needs quality content when you have good ads? But those in-text ads don't take any space on the website; they don't cover real estate.

In-text ads just blend smoothly into the content, so they actually force us to come up with original content. It's terrible!

6.   No new unrelated topics.

It's nice that the ads around a website's content throw in different ideas that are unrelated to the content. You can read a historic post about The Manhattan Project, while the banners announce the new season of *Project Runway.* It opens the mind to new horizons. Those nasty in-text ads are hooked on an actual term within the content, so the ads are mostly relevant and supplement the content. With in-text relevancy, how will people get exposed to new topics?

7.   We're addicted to ad interruptions.

We breathe ads. From the moment we wake up—and go on our way to work or school, sit in our office or classroom, and watch TV or work on the PC—until we close our eyes to sleep (and sometimes even in our dreams), advertisers fight for our attention, interrupting us no matter what we're doing. In-text ads are different. The double-underline links tell us there's an ad behind them and ask for our permission. We give it a hover, and only if we're interested in the ad within the bubble do we click on it. In-text ads are not stuck to our faces. But hey, we're used to ads everywhere. If all advertisements ask for our permission, we might miss those precious interruptions. Don't we need those interruptions like the air we breathe?

8.   Nobody likes advertisers.

People generally don't like advertisers and marketers. Sad but true. In-text ads get high quality scores from advertisers. It makes sense. Since the visitor actually gives permission to be exposed to the ad and actively demonstrates interest (by hovering and clicking), there's a good chance the visitor will be genuinely interested in the advertiser's content. From the advertiser's point of view, it's the next best thing after search ads and way better than banners and contextual ads around the content. When you use in-text ads, you make advertisers happy, and why would you want to do that?

9. You need to analyze effective cost per mille (eCPM) and click-through rate (CTR).

Do you prefer getting paid without work-related incentives? If so, stay away from in-text ads. Integrating in-text ads into your website is very easy, and money comes in instantly. But then, you can always earn more with simple changes. Consider the color, the format of the underline, the number of hooks, the location in the page, blacklist keywords, and white-list keywords. Improvements like these take little work and can add up on your bottom line. But alas, to get these higher revenue numbers, you need to look at your eCPM and CTR and analyze some data. Doubling your money is possible, but if you're afraid of some work, you'd better keep your distance.

The Top 10 in-text Ad Advantages

Now that I've come up with the Top 9 reasons *not* to use in-text ads and given you ammunition against your in-text-loving friends, you might even find yourself joining them. So let's look at the Top 10 advantages and benefits of in-text ads. The issues are quite similar, but the angle of view is reversed. I also deal with most of these issues elsewhere in more depth, but this list can prove to be handy as an overview.

1. In-text ads are quiet.

We got used to reading text continuously online, even when there was a hyperlink over a few words. That's how the Internet was built. The double-underline links are no different. They don't stop or disturb our flow of reading. As opposed to banners that tend to be graphically noisy with many colors and animation, and sometimes even literally noisy with sound, in-text ads are subtle additions to the original content. As website publishers, we strive to keep a good balance between content and "noise," and in-text ads are a good choice in that regard.

2. A good source of additional revenue.

In-text ads generate extra revenue from a website without affecting other sources of income. When considering your website monetization plan, remember that in-text ads represent an additional source of income that can be as high as Google AdSense in some cases. Before flooding a website with complex affiliate programs and jumpy full-page ads, publishers should give in-text ads a try. The stable monthly payment from their in-text ad provider has become a cornerstone of website revenue for many website publishers.

3. The one-minute integration of in-text ads.

Integrating in-text ads into a website is so easy that even I managed to do it. It can take less than a minute to simply paste a line of code into the website, and that's it! The in-text ads are there automatically. This is one of the only money-making additions to a website that does not require changes to the website, any development, or IT work. Giving it a try and seeing the revenue accumulate is actually easier than writing a new post or updating your Facebook page.

4. In-text ads are pay-per-click.

Most in-text ads are on a pay-per-click basis (PPC), and the website publisher gets paid for every click. We sometimes put so much effort into affiliate programs with pay-per-lead (CPL) or pay-per-acquisition (CPA) models that we forget the joy of PPC. Every visitor that clicks on an ad earns you revenue. Even the Google AdSense Link Units require two clicks to earn something, but many websites still use them. This is a clear advantage that calls for in-text ads to come early in the game.

5. Focus on good content.

I had a conversation with a major newspaper publisher regarding his online edition, and he said that writers claim that in-text ads disrespect their editorial professionalism. A quick look on the website revealed a DoubleClick ad unit with a flash banner of a completely naked woman inviting the reader to have sex with her right now (from AdultFriendFinder). How can this lady's offer be more respectful, I asked, than a double-underline link over an important keyword within the content? He had to agree. In-text ads complete and supplement good content and keep the ads relevant to the main focus of the reader.

6. In-text ads don't use real estate.

All web designers now follow the Apple approach of empty spaces and white areas to draw readers to the actual content. Since they attach themselves to the content, in-text ads don't use any real estate on a website. As such, they leave the designer the option to choose where to place banners and where to leave blanks for virtual air to flow through. This design benefit of in-text ads is a major factor when comparing them to many other monetization and advertising methods.

7. In-text ads are relevant.

In-text ads are hooked on actual terms within the content, so they are mostly relevant and supplement the content. First, they're much more relevant than contextual banners around the text. Second, relevancy is in the eye of the advertiser. The great feedback from advertisers with regard to in-text ads proves that the matching algorithms work well. By the way, when a top Alexa 1,000-website editor told me that she got a complaint from a visitor about an irrelevant ad, I had to tell her that it was great news. Receiving a single complaint out of many thousands of community members speaks strongly about the relevancy that the vast majority of visitors find with in-text ads.

8. In-text ads are a form of permission marketing.

The marketing guru Seth Godin has set the stage for modern marketing by focusing advertisers on permission marketing: When a potential customer *permits* the advertiser to bring his message to the forefront, the potential for conversion is high. While most online advertising techniques try to interrupt people from their online activities—like TV ads in the middle of a show—in-text ads don't open unless the visitor expressly requests more information. The mouse hover is an intended action that reveals a small ad within the bubble, and the click on it is a second active request, representing double permission. Integrating in-text ads means that you respect your online visitors by not interrupting them unless they have genuine interest in the ad content.

9. Advertisers like in-text ads.

In-text ads get high-quality scores from advertisers. In my experience, since the visitor actually gives permission to be exposed to the ad, chances are high that he will be genuinely interested in the advertiser's content. This is the next best thing after search ads, and advertisers that analyze return on their advertising budgets find in-text ads to be rewarding. When advertisers are happy with in-text ads, budgets grow, the payment per click increases, and the overall eCPM gets better.

10. Optimizing in-text ads gets real results.

While it's true that adding in-text ads to your site takes only a minute, there's much more that you can do to improve your earning results. Consider the color, the format of the underline, the number of hooks, the location on the page, blacklist keywords, whitelist keywords, and more. When you analyze your eCPM and CTR and act according to some of these optimization tips, you can even double your revenue. Without a third party to optimize your ads, this is an important factor for professionals.

10 Advantages and Counting

The more I work with in-text ads, the more I'm convinced that this method of website monetization is highly beneficial to the three points of the triangle—publishers, advertisers, and readers. I'm sure that with time, even more benefits will emerge. Perhaps some problems too, of course. I'm inviting you to join the conversation and contribute from your experience on my blog at OnlineSiesta.com.

CHAPTER 3:
TECHNOLOGY BASICS OF IN-TEXT ADVERTISING

In order to better understand in-text advertising, some technological background is required. I won't dive into the code structure here; I'm not the right person to attempt that. But it's important to know the basics because the leading in-text ad networks utilize different technology, so the following analysis may be helpful in choosing the right partner for you.

The Magic of a Little JavaScript

When you integrate in-text ads on your website, all you're required to do is insert a little piece of JavaScript code. This invisible code, when run by a browser, calls upon a bigger script to run on your website and identify your website to the in-text ad provider.

The first job for this code is to analyze the content of the page and determine if it's suitable for in-text ads. Sometimes, if there isn't enough text, or if the text is not suitable for advertising, the process will stop right there with no ads being placed. If the page is suitable, the code will then analyze the page's content and identify the terms that get the highest scores for balancing the contextual relevancy and the potential for advertising. The top terms will be highlighted as double-underline links and will serve as hooks for the advertisements.

As explained before, if a user is interested to learn more about a highlighted hook, he can hover over it with the mouse, and a bubble will appear with a relevant ad inside. The code is asked to match the ad to the reader and to the term in order to maximize the chances for a click. If a click is made, the code needs to send the reader to the advertiser's landing page and monitor behavior in order to charge the advertiser and credit the website publisher for the ad's current price.

All of this magic begins with that little piece of JavaScript code, but it requires a robust and smart system behind it. This system has several key differentiators among the leading in-text ad providers.

Timing of the Load

When the JavaScript is loaded and the bigger code is called into action, the browser has some work to do. Therefore, the timing of the load is important. If this work is done in parallel with the loading of the page, it may slow down the loading of the page's content. Such slowdown could result in the loss of visitors as they become frustrated and leave the page before it finishes loading. The natural conclusion is that it's important to make sure that the script you're using only runs *after* your page has finished loading the main content.

These days, with the numerous types of widgets and other scripts that run on a page, there's another timing factor to consider—the timing of the in-text script among other scripts. The best example would be the common Google Analytics script, which runs in order to count the visitors and monitor their behavior on your website. Since the Google Analytics code may take some time to load as well, if you place the in-text script after it, the ads may appear a little later. The same goes for other widgets. It's up to you as a publisher to determine which code should run first. My recommendation is to place the in-text JavaScript just after the actual page's content but before other scripts that are not money-oriented.

Dynamic in-text Ad Placement

The most challenging aspect of in-text advertising involves the hook and matching the best ad to the visitor. This process of ad placement requires analyzing many factors, including the context of the page, the content category of the website, the known characteristics of the users, the highlighted term within the hook, and the available advertising campaigns at that specific moment. Since the web is very dynamic, some of these factors may change every minute or even within a given minute. Available ads and their prices are mostly handled through open markets, and they change all the time.

Some in-text ad providers do not use dynamic ad placement. I won't point them out, but it's quite easy to check if the selected hooks and the shown ads change when you hit refresh. Ad networks that have relatively old technology may find it difficult to dynamically match the ads, so they actually place the ads beforehand without maximizing their revenue potential. In fact, some of them even manually choose the hooks for highlighting, so they won't deal well with dynamic content found in blogs, forums, and news websites.

Automation Level and Organizational Structure

At Infolinks, we made automation a top priority. The smarter the algorithm and the more automated the in-text ad placing process, the higher the effective cost-per-mille (eCPM) is for the website publisher. There are two reasons for that. First, automated processes are more sensitive to changes in the market and to dynamic content; they simply get better results. Second, automated processes allow you to manage the system with minimal staff, focusing human resources on customer service. When the highlighted hooks require manual content analysis, the organizational structure has higher costs that limit the organization's ability to share most of the revenue with the publisher.

Again, this is from my own personal experience, and I'm sure other networks are striving to do the same. When we set up our system to require minimal manual intervention, we saved money and enabled our organization to offer a higher revenue share to our publishers. This is a good example of technology differences that have an immediate influence on publishers.

IT Infrastructure

Another example of technology differences is hidden within the IT infrastructure. Anyone who has worked for a web-related company knows that IT costs—the prices of computers, servers, and networks—climb so high that they become a major factor in the company's finances. Placing in-text ads requires real-time analysis of content and real-time matching of ads in rapidly changing market conditions. If the system is not built to take the IT infrastructure into consideration, IT costs can make it impossible for the company to share most of the revenue with its publishers.

In-text Ads May Look the Same

While in-text ads may appear to work like magic with a little bit of code, there's actually a lot of work behind them. Also, while most in-text ads may appear to work similarly, there are major differences among in-text ad networks, and understanding those differences will help you choose the right partner. If you're looking for deeper insights into the technological process, drop me a line, and I will try to get you the answer from someone on our tech team. If you need more help with understanding the business implications of these technological differences, I might even try answering you myself …

Chapter 4:

Advanced Website Monetization with In-Text Ads

Website Monetization Tip #1:
Use Double-Underline
Distinction and Temptation

Despite the temptation of a short-term increase in your click-through rate, avoid hiding in-text links, and use a distinct format like double-underline.

The hooks—those hyperlinks that yield a bubble upon mouse hover—are the key to website monetization with in-text ads. When the provider's algorithm works well, the keywords selected for hooks will be of interest to the reader and relevant to the content. When a reader is interested in the highlighted term, she will hover over it with the mouse, consider the ad within the bubble, and click if she wants to learn more. That's where the cash lies.

The reader can also choose to click on the hook directly, however. Such a direct click will also lead to the advertiser's landing page and generate the per-click revenue. And here's the temptation: Hooks for in-text ads can be formatted as regular links with the same format and appearance as other links on the page, such as the single-underline format previously mentioned. When disguised as regular links, readers may click on the hooks without knowing that they lead to paid-for content. Again, in the short term, this leads to more clicks per page views (higher click-through rate or CTR), and it can generate higher revenue on a pay-per-click basis (PPC).

The Catch

But remember that there's a catch! This will only work for the short term. The obvious explanation is that the website's readers will soon learn that not all links are regular, so they will either avoid clicking entirely or screen them carefully with a hover. This way, after the first increase in clicks, there will be a drop. I've seen this happen with many websites. Now I know some website publishers are smiling to themselves, thinking, "Well, I don't manage to get repeat visitors anyway, so at least I'll get a paid click out of them on that single visit." Sorry, but this is a wrong assumption too.

The deeper reasoning behind this tip—to use a distinct format for ad links—covers both repeating and new visitors. When a reader clicks on a link expecting to go to another related article but lands instead on an advertiser's page, she usually goes immediately back to the original page, or just shuts down the window if it's a new window. A disguised ad is an interruption to reading, so it's mostly ignored and even frowned upon. From the advertiser's point of view, this is the worst kind of click. First, the advertiser paid for that click but didn't get the expected attention when the reader simply left the ad's landing page immediately. Second, and much worse, the visitor may even leave with a negative feeling toward the brand that managed to fool her into clicking.

Losing Revenue and Happiness

When advertisers are unhappy with the clicks they pay for, they pull the campaign from the website. This can be done specifically against a website that repeatedly sends bouncing visitors (those visitors that leave immediately). And if you think smaller websites can hide below the radar, think again. Automatic filters give small websites low-quality scores and block them out as well.

Once advertisers pull their campaigns from a certain website, the ads get lower and lower click value, so the effective revenue (eCPM) drops. In fact, even the click-through rate decreases, as the active campaigns become more general, and the ads become much less relevant and interesting to the site's readers.

If all of this is not convincing enough, add to it the general frustration your visitors feel when they're tricked into clicking on an ad. Is that the user experience you're aiming for? And think about it: Which of the formats—regular or double-underline links—is more noticeable and has a chance to get your own interest and click?

The Tip: Distinct Format for Ad Links

My tip is this: Use a distinct format for in-text ads. When your visitors recognize the hooks as a signal to an ad, they can easily disregard them and not be interrupted while reading. When the hook is interesting, however, they know there's a bubble behind it, so they hover, consider the ad, and actively give their permission to be exposed to the advertiser's content. Clicks that come with permission are highly valuable to advertisers, and they will reward them with good feedback. This positive feedback will soon be translated into higher value per click and eventually into higher revenue. In professional terms, you may experience a lower CTR, but the eCPM and bottom-line revenue will be higher. You will then have more available clicks for other uses (like content-related links), and, most importantly, your website's general user experience will be improved. Don't we all like happy visitors?

The Added Value of Double-Underline

One last thing. Why double-underline? This tip is about making a clear distinction between the in-text ad links and other hyperlinks on the page. Any distinct format will do. Double-underline will do even better.

Using double-underline has an important added value. More and more people online recognize this format as unique to in-text advertising. All of the advantages of making both your visitors and advertisers happy by getting permission for clicks are leveraged by using a common format that doesn't annoy your visitors and doesn't distract their focus away from your content. I recommend sticking to the standard of the online community, so noticeable double-underline it is.

Website Monetization Tip #2: Choosing the Text Ad's Color, *The Color of Money*

The color of the ad links on your website's pages has a significant impact on your potential revenue. Choosing the right color for your ad links contributes to this distinction, but there's much more to it.

The color of the in-text links should stand out from the text just enough to clearly present the link as an advertisement, but the color shouldn't stand out *too much* so that it avoids interruption to smooth reading.

The chosen color also needs to be part of the overall color palette of your website. In other words, protect your tasteful design! in-text ads become part of the website's general appearance, so the color should match the surrounding environment. There's no magic matching formula, however. Some people like pink and brown together, while others think it's hideous. So the choice is up to you or your designer to consider the general design of the website when choosing the ads' color, not just money-making considerations. Good design will contribute to the user experience and user satisfaction, which is crucial to your website and business.

Choosing Your Color

Here's the practical tip: Choose quickly, and then choose again. And again. Yup, that's the way. When you first integrate in-text ads, take a look at your website, and choose a color that you think will work. Don't think too much. If you don't like making such quick choices, simply stick with the default color.

Then get some feedback. Ask your team, friends, and visitors for their opinions about the color. Based on the feedback and your own taste, change the color. This should be very easy to do through your account with your in-text ad provider.

After you change the color, give it another few days, and compare the statistics. In most cases, your in-text stats will provide you with a clear picture. Look for changes in the percentage of clicks out of your page impressions (click-through rate or CTR). Check the eCPM and bottom-line revenue as well.

More money equals right color choice in most cases. But don't test it for just one day. That may simply indicate visitors' interest in the new color—nothing more. If there's no change in the statistics, it's back to your personal taste. And if you're still not sure, change the color again. It's a click of a button and free of charge. Keep changing it until you find the right match—a color that gets you the clicks and revenue you want, matches your website's overall appearance, and doesn't interrupt smooth reading.

Extra Tip: Image and Video Sites

If the website or pages that you're analyzing for color choice focus on images or video, your visitors will most likely disregard the accompanying text. In-text ads usually yield a lower volume of clicks and revenue on pages like these. Still, it doesn't mean that you can't enjoy the extra income. For web pages with images or video, try eye-catching colors that get your visitors' attention. While your visitors watch a video or view an image, they're usually looking for their next click—so make sure that the ad links are easily identified. Then you shouldn't have to worry about interrupting smooth reading since most visitors don't read the entire text anyway. Just make those links shine!

Website Monetization Tip #3:
In-Text Ads On and Off,
In-Text Ads—Not on Every Word

When you add in-text ads, a smart algorithm analyzes the content on your web pages and highlights the keywords and terms with the best match to the page's content and potential advertising. Still, no one knows and understands your own content as well as you. With some help, the in-text algorithm can improve its performance, and the results will show up in your website monetization reports. The nice surprise here is that it's very easy. All you have to do is recognize areas and terms that are better left alone and not highlighted as in-text ad links.

Website Areas to Avoid

Some areas on your web pages are just unsuitable for in-text ads. Here are some examples:

1. Fixed content areas—headers and footers, navigation bars.

2. Fixed content pages—the About and Contact pages.

3. Repeating sections—the Details area in a forum, the Add Comment paragraph in a blog.

Let's face it: When your visitors read the Contact page or actually review the footer, they're not likely to actively choose to be exposed to an advertisement. If they do click an ad link there, it's probably a mistake, and they will hit the back button, become annoyed, and lower your chances for future visits and revenue.

Since the number of hooks (In-Text ad links) on a certain web page is usually limited to a set number, highlighting terms in areas where visitors will not regard or click them is truly a waste of hooks. Such misplaced hooks replace better placed hooks and reduce your potential monetization.

Specific Terms to Avoid

In addition to unwanted areas, there are also specific keywords and terms that are better left out of the in-text ad algorithm's way.

First, there are repeating terms. You know which terms appear repeatedly on your pages but are not relevant for ad text links. Think about it. Here are a few examples:

1. Automated Text—Found mostly in blogs and forums: "posted by," "date," and other terms that are automatically added very often.

2. Names, places, and subject matter names are sometimes used very often but are not good candidates for ad text links.

Second, there are specifically problematic keywords. A friend of mine runs an informational website about protecting children on the web and avoiding various online risks. On a certain page, the term *pornography* can appear several times, even though the subject is how to filter it out and protect children from exposure. In certain cases, an in-text ad algorithm can recognize pornography as the subject of the page but disregard the negative context. Still, my friend prefers not to highlight *pornography* on her pages.

Then there are misleading ad links. If your website promotes an e-book, video, or software for downloading, your page probably includes descriptive words and sentences like "Download here." These sentences are not the actual download links, but they are part of the page's content. Since the page is, in fact, about downloads, the algorithm may highlight these terms for ads, but your visitors may mistake an ad link for the download button. These clicks are double trouble. You lose the download click you wanted in the first place, and the advertiser gets a mistaken click that he doesn't like, probably rewarding you with low-quality feedback and a long-term decrease in revenue.

Each website has its own potentially harmful terms. Which keywords are better left alone on your websites?

As smart as the algorithm can be, terms that appear often seem to be important to the page's content. Despite efforts to automatically recognize irrelevant words and avoid them, there are so many different ways to create a website, blog, or forum that it's practically impossible to cover them all. Just a little help from you can do wonders to improve the algorithm's performance, as well as your monetization potential.

How to Choose Better in-text Ads

By avoiding certain unwanted areas and keywords on your website, you can actually help the in-text ad algorithm to choose better keywords and increase your potential website monetization. As promised earlier, it's surprisingly easy to do. You simply mark which areas and keywords you want to keep out of the in-text algorithm's reach.

For whole areas, there are simple HTML tags for turning the algorithm on and off. With each in-text provider, there are slight differences, but all of the big providers have this option available. Pick up the exact tag formation from your provider, and mark as "Off" any areas that should not have in-text ads in them. Don't forget to add the "On" tag afterward and test it a little to make sure that the ads appear in the right places and are missing from the indicated areas.

For unwanted keywords, there should be a "blacklist." Ask your in-text provider about it, and create your website's list. Coming up with the initial list shouldn't be too difficult, and you can always edit it and add more keywords to it later. In fact, you can prepare this list right now and immediately improve your earnings within a matter of minutes.

Website Monetization Tip #4:
In-Text Ads—Open in New Window,
To Open or Not to Open in a New Window

Some website publishers ask if they can open an in-text ad's landing page in a new browser window. The answer is yes, it's possible from a technical standpoint, but it isn't a good practice. If you really feel you must do so, ask your provider to set your in-text ads to open in a new window, but please read the next paragraphs first to give me a chance to discourage you.

What is a new window? Any hyperlink leads to a new web page. The link can be customized to either open the targeted web page within the same active window of the browser, replacing the original page, or open it in a new browser window, leaving the current browser window open along with the original page. In other words, it either replaces the current page (same window) or keeps the current page open (new window). When designing your website, you need to determine how to configure all of your links—open in the same window or in a new window—and there are many discussions about this subject that I will leave for others. But I will, of course, discuss it with respect to your in-text ads.

Can a Visitor Stay Forever?

It's important to understand that no visitor stays on your website forever. Eventually, as much as they like your content, they will move on to another site, close their browser, run out of electricity, go out, go to sleep, or maybe, sadly, pass away. So why not prepare for it? Give your visitors a good exit experience, together with a good reason to come back and bring others with them. Forcing a visitor to stay by technical means will not keep her forever anyway, and it will probably worsen her experience and her overall feeling toward your website.

So there's no reason to mourn departed visitors. Rather than having them leave with no good-bye, it's better to have them leave through a relevant ad with a click that generates you some revenue.

Advertisers Ask for Attention and Pay for It

Have you wondered why advertisers are willing to pay you for each click? Apart from how nice you are, they actually need your visitors' attention. When they planned their landing page, their ads, and their advertising budget, they had some goals in mind that require the clicking visitor to actually give attention to their ad's landing page. Embrace this fact; don't fight it.

When a website publisher asks to open the ad's landing page in a new window, he does so because he doesn't want to lose the visitor. But face it: This is exactly what the advertiser wants—your visitors' full attention to the ad's message. When you make it easier for your visitor to leave the ad's landing page and go back to your page, you hurt the advertiser's goal. When advertisers are unhappy with the conversion they get from your visitors, they won't want to work with you. Through automatic processes, advertisers will stay away from your website, and you won't even notice it at first. But your website will get ads that pay less and that are less interesting to your visitors. With time, your site's user experience will diminish, and your revenue will decrease.

When the ad's landing page opens in the same window, the user gets a more natural web surfing experience, and the landing page has a better chance of getting the user's attention. When you open the ad's landing page in a new window, the user is less likely to give the same amount of focused attention to the advertiser's message.

The Back Button

If you adhere to my recommendations above and let advertisers get the attention they pay for, your in-text ad revenue will grow. If your site visitors ask why your ads don't open in a new window, you can always point them to that arrow-shaped button which reverses time—the back button. Once they've looked at the ad's landing page, they can choose to proceed to wherever the advertiser has suggested (buy a book, for example) or simply hit the back button and return to your original web page.

Note that sometimes the back button doesn't work. Due to the complex path that the browser goes through from click to landing page, or due to the advertiser's configuration, the back button may not be an option. Although providers try to prevent this from happening and keep the back button enabled, it's sometimes impossible to avoid the problem with various browsers and advertisers.

In cases of no back button or when the visitor simply likes the advertiser's landing page and stays there, your website should be attractive enough to entice users to come back to it voluntarily. That's the right way to keep your visitors, not by some technical means.

Website Monetization Tip #5:
Of Browsers and in-text Ads,
Earn More from a Website by Knowing the Browser

Getting to know your audience is a major part of any plan to make money from a website, and it's no secret that a visitor's choice of browser can tell you something about the expected behavior of that visitor. So to increase your earnings from in-text ads, you can take specific actions related to your visitors' browsers that can make a difference. An analysis of general statistics from in-text advertising reveals a few interesting insights that I'm happy to share with you.

Internet Explorer, Firefox, Chrome, and Safari

This website monetization tip is based on the browsing statistics of thousands of websites with integrated in-text ads, focusing on the four major Internet browsers: Internet Explorer, Firefox, Chrome, and Safari. Clearly, as with any statistical analysis, the lessons from this research are limited because they're generalized, and you might find that your website visitors behave differently. Still, there is much to learn from information gathered from large volumes of traffic.

In the data used here from a single day in December 2009, Internet Explorer users counted for almost half of the page views, Firefox users represented 35 percent of the page views, Chrome was used for 7 percent of the total traffic, Safari users viewed 5 percent of the pages, and the remaining 3 percent of web pages were mostly viewed on Opera. While web surfing behavior is different in India than it is in Canada, for example, the data here was analyzed without referring to the location of the users. Also, while analyzing data from a longer period could tell us even more, the data here included many millions of page views, which should be enough to reach a few conclusions.

Targeting Safari Users Can Earn You More

Mac users with the Safari browser seem to be a unique group that tends toward graphics and design. In this analysis, they represent a smaller group with two major differences from the other users and with a promise for higher revenue.

The first finding is a little disappointing: The fill rate for Safari users reached only 75 percent of the general fill rate. The term "fill rate" means the number of viewed pages where the in-text ad script has managed to highlight double-underline hooks, excluding business-related decisions, so it only relates to the influence of technology. The explanation for the lower number of pages could be found in ad blockers or other scripts that interfere with the in-text script, but other reasons could also be relevant. From the publisher's point of view, this means that you should expect less page views with in-text ads from these users, which could lead to lower earnings.

But there is a nice surprise regarding Safari visitors: They yield higher payments per click. In fact, the cost-per-click (CPC) paid by advertisers for clicks from Safari browsers was nearly 50 percent higher than the general cost per click. Why is that? It seems that Mac users are highly sought after by online advertisers, and the competition drives prices up. These high prices compensate for the lower fill rate, and Safari users measured by effective CPM get the top levels of earnings.

The conclusion is that targeting Safari users is a viable strategy for making money online, as long as you understand that they are limited in number compared to the overall online population and generate lower page volumes with in-text ads. How to attract those lucrative Safari users is a different story to be discussed elsewhere, but delivering content about Mac is a sure bet for doing so and getting high CPC clicks.

Internet Explorer is the King of in-text Ad Revenue

Visitors who use Microsoft's Internet Explorer stand at the top of most categories relevant to earning more with in-text ads on your website. First, they represent the largest group of users, and while Explorer is losing market share to competing browsers, it's still the clear leader. Second, these users simply click more often. The click-through rate on in-text ads measured for Explorer users is more than 54 percent higher than for users of others browsers. Third, and most important, the effective CPM from Explorer users is influenced by the high volume of clicks and, therefore, much higher than the expected website revenue from users of other browsers. Actually, this is an understatement. In the data sampled here, the eCPM measured was 85 percent higher!

Why does an Explorer user click more often on in-text ads? The answer to this crucial question is hidden somewhere in the identity of the users themselves. Since most personal computers are still sold bundled with Microsoft's Windows operating system and Internet Explorer browsers, using a different browser requires an active choice. It makes sense to assume that users who are less web savvy won't make that choice and will simply stick with the default. Apparently there is a direct correlation between your level of web expertise and your willingness to click on online advertising ... or at least click on in-text ads.

The conclusions from this data can be taken into consideration on both the targeting level and the technology level or the type of integration you use. On the targeting level, delivering content aimed at users who are less "webby" could prove to be worth it, and it's up to you to analyze what content they are looking for. From the technology aspect, a website publisher can prioritize in-text ads for Explorer users by identifying these users and running the in-text script earlier in the website's loading or adding more hooks for the ads. You can ask your in-text ad provider for ideas as to how to optimize your website for higher monetization results.

There are additional interesting differences among the different versions of Internet Explorer. For example, the newer the version, the higher the CPC. These results can be explained by external factors that are not directly related to the browser, however. It could be that Microsoft manages to generate upgrades to the newer versions of Explorer faster in markets with higher broadband penetration, and such markets probably have stronger online advertising markets.

Firefox Users Generate Less Website Revenue

Firefox users earn less in-text revenue for website publishers. This fact is not surprising if you think about who these users are. Making the active decision to switch from the default Explorer to Firefox is probably more common for users who have likes and dislikes about the web. These users click only about two-thirds as often as Explorer users. Firefox users install add-ons to block ads, surf more, and generate more page views. As a result, they may become more annoyed by ads. Whatever the reasons, they click less.

It's important to realize that if your website typically attracts "webby" visitors with a tendency toward Firefox, your monetization results from in-text ads will be lower. My best recommendation is to explain the nature of in-text ads to these users. Make sure that your visitors know that the double-underline ad links on your website are there to help you finance better content for them, keep it free when possible, and to avoid intrusive, jumping banners. By clarifying the advantages of in-text ads to your users, you may generate genuine interest in these ads and, therefore, more clicks. This can easily be done by a sidebar link to an FAQ explaining the nature of in-text ads. Consider a link saying "Double-Underline Explained" or something to that effect. As for technological improvements, you can optimize the appearance of in-text ads to match the taste shown by your Firefox users. For this, you need to first get to know them better and use the flexibility of your in-text provider.

Chrome Users Follow Firefox Patterns

Chrome users seem to follow the footsteps of Firefox users. The statistics of both groups are quite similar: They click less than Explorer users and yield lower in-text ad revenue. The similarity of results for Firefox and Chrome users teaches us that Chrome users are more or less the same users. Currently Chrome users still represent a small group, but it would be worthwhile to study them further as this group grows and develops its own unique behavior patterns.

Earn More with in-text Ads

The bottom line is that getting to know the differences between visitors according to their choice of web browser could help you to increase your revenue from in-text ads. There is still much to learn, however. For example, iPhone and other mobile phone browsers show other surfing patterns, but this seems to stem from the different user experience on the mobile phone and not only from the choice of browser. Getting to know your website's visitors and acting upon the findings to optimize the user experience and the in-text ad integration is an important part of your website monetization plan. Even if you're not yet ready to run different scripts according to your users' browsers, you should at least explain the nature of in-text ads to your site visitors. It could help with Firefox and Chrome surfers, and in the long run this will improve the overall quality and results from all users.

Chapter 5:
In-Text Advertising Networks and Providers

Choosing the Best in-text Ad Network

And the winner for Best in-text Ad Network is ... Well, did you really expect that it would be that simple? While I can easily name the nominees for Best in-text Ad Network Award and detail the important aspects to compare before choosing your provider, there's only one name I can put on the winner's pedestal with sound mind. I just can't write it here.

As I stated before, I work at Infolinks, and this is where I collected my experience about in-text advertising. If I were going to recommend a single company, it would have to be Infolinks (especially if I want to keep my job). But I will keep my writing professional and avoid a direct recommendation. I will, however, point out the important issues and help you to make your choice.

The Top 3 in-text Ad Networks

The top three in-text ad networks are Kontera, Vibrant Media, and Infolinks. Each of these providers has proven stability over time, and you can count on all of them to deliver ads around the clock and pay you on time every month.

Kontera holds the title for being the first in-text ad network. While there were other companies dealing with in-text services before Kontera, this company was the first to offer a commercial service that was based purely on in-text advertising. As a direct competitor, I can't dive into the details of how good it is or the problems with its service. The objective facts, however, are that it was the first out there, but its growth slowed down when competition arrived.

Vibrant Media started offering its in-text ad services after Kontera had already established a strong hold on the market. Nevertheless, it has managed to bypass Kontera with big publishers, and this has become its focus. While Kontera is responsible for putting in-text ads in the hearts of many publishers, Vibrant Media is responsible for penetrating larger websites and turning this method into a legitimate advertising format.

Infolinks was the third to join this triple-headed race, but with the fastest growth rate it has gained a very positive reputation among publishers who have compared earning results among the three providers. It seems that our team's efforts in monetizing more pages than other providers, achieving top click-through rates, and gaining higher bottom-line revenue didn't go unnoticed, and the faster growth rate and blog posts with comparisons attest to these advantages.

In light of the above, choosing Kontera, Vibrant Media, or Infolinks would be a reasonable choice. As far as I know, both Kontera and Vibrant Media require an exclusive commitment of twelve months at the point of entry and don't accept smaller websites, while Infolinks offers a much more flexible contract to all websites with an option to try the service, modify it, and even leave it at will. If I didn't work at Infolinks, this would probably be my reason for recommending it to people who are new to in-text ads. If you already work with an in-text ad provider, you can simply compare results and ask around the Google planet to help you make your choice.

Non-Focused in-text Ad Providers

A few online advertising networks added in-text lines of service to their existing display and textual offers. Networks like AdBrite, Affinity, and Chitika include in-text ads as part of their offered services.

However, as far as I can see, many publishers who work with these networks for their banners or widgets still choose to work with one of the top in-text ad providers. The reason for that seems to be focus. When a company's focus is elsewhere, you can't expect much of its other services. Therefore, unless a publisher finds an enormous advantage in getting several services from the same provider, he won't choose a non-focused in-text ad network.

Small and Niche in-text Ad Networks

After the success of the top in-text advertising networks, a few startup companies jumped into this market as well with in-text offers. Writing a script that highlights terms within existing content is no longer a major hurdle to climb over. But in-text advertising has a lot more to it, and it isn't as easy as it may seem. Building an in-text ad network requires much more. Analyzing content to find the most relevant terms—matching ads that will gain a high click-through rate and yield high eCPM and real revenue, all the while withstanding substantial traffic in real time—takes a lot of knowledge, execution, and resources.

Some of the smaller entrants like MediaText have already closed shop, and this could, unfortunately, happen to others. I still haven't seen a report about any small in-text ad network that has managed to provide a stable service or get anywhere near the top networks. But my entrepreneurial heart has a soft spot for new startups, so I do hope that some of them will rise to the top. At this stage, however, I can't recommend any small network, and trying one of them is a risk that you should take only with your eyes wide open.

There have been a few attempts to take over a specific content niche that other providers either won't enter or don't specialize in. The best example is adult-oriented websites, which the top in-text ad networks won't accept. The two networks that do allow adult-oriented websites (even hardcore porn websites) are Clicksor and AdBrite (under its black label which isn't really separated from its core business). If you're in that kind of business, one of these networks would probably be your choice for in-text ads.

International / Foreign Language in-text Providers

If you operate a website in Polish, your only choice to monetize your content with in-text ads is the Polish brand, Smart Context (www.smartcontext.pl). As far as I know, this is the only in-text provider that works in the Polish language, and since my Polish is a little rusty, I can't really examine its service to recommend or criticize it. If your website is in Spanish, Infolinks should be your choice for in-text ads monetization, as it is the leader in this market. If your website is in German or French, both Vibrant Media and Infolinks can help you with in-text ad monetization. With time, I'm sure that additional languages will be covered by solutions from both the leading networks and new entrants.

The international market is not only foreign languages, however. Most English websites have many visitors that are not from the United States of America, including countries like Canada, England, Australia, New Zealand, and India. From my experience, out of the top three in-text ad networks, Infolinks is the only provider to offer ads to all international traffic. While the expected CPC in these markets is lower, there's still money to be earned, and if you have substantial international traffic, this is a major factor to consider. My recommendation here, again, is to simply ask the provider about international coverage.

As much as I like in-text advertising, I'm not sure that running networks solely for in-text ads will be justified in the long term. As an emerging new advertising method, in-text services must be provided by unique players. These focused efforts are the power behind the penetration and market trust. However, as this method matures, it will join other types of online advertising, and as such, consolidation is almost visible at the horizon. This happened before in other industries and with other types of online ads. It isn't unlikely to assume that the giant players in the online industry will want a piece of this fast-growing and proven market. When they do, the wisest step for them will be to use the experience that the existing in-text ad networks have gained. Will this happen? Who knows?

CHAPTER 6:
IN-TEXT ADVERTISING REVENUE AND EARNINGS

How Much Money Can You Earn With in-text Ads?

This is the most frequent question I get from website publishers before they integrate in-text ads for the first time. They say that they understand that in-text ads are fast, relevant, subtle, don't take space, and don't require changes, but they want to know how much they can earn from these ads. I wish I could answer this with a number, such as $12,430 per month, but it just isn't that simple. I can answer, however, with some rules and a simple formula to calculate your website's potential in-text revenue. It will take some basic terminology clarification and further analysis, but bear with me: I promise a formula that you can easily use.

Breaking Down eCPM

Most often, online revenue is measured in eCPM—effective Cost-Per-Mille (thousand) is the original term—and, as expected, it can be highly misleading. So let's linger with it for a paragraph. This acronym simply stands for your bottom-line revenue divided by your relevant page views, and then divided by 1,000, all in the relevant currency. Why is it divided by 1,000? Because the actual number is too low. Dividing the page views helps to make the number higher and more comfortable, but it also, unfortunately, makes it much more confusing.

For example, if your website had 20,000 relevant page views

yesterday and yielded $100, your eCPM was $100 / (20,000 / 1,000) = $5. If you keep a stable average eCPM of $5 and stable traffic of an average 20,000 page views daily, your website has a potential of $3,000 in monthly revenue. (This number is obtained by multiplying $5 by your monthly page views, divided by 1,000.) So why is calculating the potential revenue so complicated? Because every one of these eCPM factors can vary widely according to your website's circumstances.

Start with Net Impressions

You know how many page views your website gets every day. Most likely, you use Google Analytics or another web analytics service or software to get this data. You may even be analyzing the hits on your servers. But this number will be different from the page views counted by your ads provider. Why? Notice that when calculating eCPM, we used the term "relevant page views," also known as "impressions" or "net impressions." As the term implies, impressions are incidents when a visitor has been exposed to the ads. Not all page views actually manage to present ads to the visitor, and, therefore, not all page views are counted as impressions.

The ratio between these relevant impressions or net impressions and the actual number of page views is sometimes called "fill rate." So if you have 100,000 page views, but only 70,000 of them are net impressions, the fill rate is 70 percent. Since the higher the number of impressions, the higher the eCPM, you clearly should aim for a high fill rate.

Where Did Your Impressions Go? Abroad!

What decreases the fill rate? Where do those precious page views go with your money? Your ad provider won't count pages that don't have ads on them. A legitimate reason might be that the visitor left so fast that while the hit on the server occurred, the page didn't finish loading all of the content and advertising scripts. Another reason might be that the page wasn't suitable for the ads. It may have had too little text to actually highlight in-text ads, or the content could have been in breach of terms, such as including adult-oriented content, which was prohibited by the provider. All of this explains why the fill rate is never 100 percent. Some page views are simply not actual net impressions.

The main reason for loss of page views, however, lies elsewhere—in geography. When advertisers purchase online campaigns, they use geo-targeting to determine where they want their ads to show up. This can be set according to IP address mapping. Your in-text ad provider may not serve ads for certain areas, cities, countries, or even whole continents. In such cases, page views from such locations where the provider didn't show ads will not be counted as part of your relevant page views or impressions, and they will not be paid for.

International Visitors Could Lead to Lost Revenue

To show how this geo-filtering can substantially affect your earnings, let's continue with the same example, but this time assume that out of the 100,000 page views, 40,000 were from the United States, while 60,000 were from Australia and Malaysia. Assume also that your in-text provider doesn't serve ads for visitors from Australia and Malaysia. In a case like this, your net impressions would be only 40,000 (40 percent fill rate), and you would earn only 40 x $5 = $200 instead of 100 x $5 = $500.

When your provider reports calculate eCPM, you would see $200 divided by 40,000 divided by 1,000, which equals $5, so it may seem as if you had the relatively high eCPM of $5 that you expected. But if you calculated your actual eCPM with your real number of page views, it would look grim: $200 divided by 100,000 divided by 1,000 equals only $2 eCPM. As you can see, comparing eCPM figures without analysis can be deceiving.

Look for the Bottom-Line Revenue

Since eCPM can hide parts of the big picture, I recommend measuring your website revenue by the bottom line in dollars (or your relevant currency). In other words, don't focus on eCPM only.

Look for an in-text ad solution that counts most of your traffic. While it is legitimate to filter out page views from areas with no ads, this is often stretched way too far to disqualify any visitor who is not from the United States. Such over-filtering will artificially increase your eCPM, but it will also lower your bottom-line revenue.

In the example above, if you manage to increase the fill rate from 40 percent to 70 percent by finding a provider or a deal that serves ads to international visitors, your eCPM will seem to be lower since the per-click payment in such locations is usually lower, but your bottom-line revenue will be higher.

Hmmm … So the per-click payment (PPC) matters too? Of course! All parameters count. The eCPM, net impressions, CPC, and CTR all count. Optimizing your website's monetization takes some work, but this work pays off. At the end of the day, it helps you keep your visitors happy with better content and a better user experience. I will continue this discussion until I get to a formula that lets you calculate how much your website can earn with in-text ads. But first, we need to talk about clicks.

Clicks Matter Most

Clicks have the highest effect on website monetization with in-text ads. Clicks on ads are what you get paid for. In most cases, in-text ads are paid on a pay-per-click basis or PPC. Although there are other models, such as pay-per-acquisition, these are usually less effective with in-text ads and will yield lower revenue. So if your revenue comes from clicks, you need to increase two parameters: first, the number of clicks, and second, the payment per click.

More Clicks and CTR

Statistically, a web page gets a certain number of clicks on in-text ads for every 100 page views. This ratio is called Click-Through Rate (CTR) and is highly important to your monetization. For example, if a page has fifteen clicks after five hundred relevant page views, this page has three clicks for every one hundred pages. So, the CTR is 3 percent. To get more clicks, you can increase the number of page views, but you should also try increasing the CTR. This will leverage the increase in page views. I will write more about increasing CTR later, but for now it's important to clarify what CTR is because it's part of the formula for estimating potential revenue.

If you know your in-text ad CTR, this number will be useful for your revenue estimation. If not, take the CTR you have on banners, and, as a thumb rule, double it. If you have textual AdSense ads on your site, you can use their CTR for now and hope it will be higher with in-text ads, or you can simply add 50 percent to it. So if your AdSense CTR is 1 percent, use 1.5 percent for this estimation.

Higher PPC

The second parameter that matters when it comes to clicks is the payment per click (PPC). From the advertiser's point of view, it's actually the cost per click (hence the term CPC), and advertisers are paying very different sums for different clicks.

When financing an online advertising campaign, an advertiser will pay more, of course, when the potential sale is higher. Therefore, the page's content niche is crucial to the PPC. A page about financial instruments and investments attracts high cost campaigns that yield high PPC, while a page about a celebrity issue with a less focused target audience normally fits only general campaigns with low PPC. And the difference can be huge. Payments per click range from fractions of a cent up to several dollars.

While the content niche highly influences the PPC on a wide

range, the entire range is subject to another crucial factor—geography. The stronger the economy, the higher the potential of sales and the costs of advertising. Therefore the higher the PPC. While the payment per click in the United States may vary between a few cents to a few dollars, the same ads in India will yield PPC rates starting from a small fraction of a cent up to a few cents only.

For estimating potential revenue, we can use a few fixed numbers, but please bear in mind that these figures are generic. Your actual numbers could be very different. So, for visitors from the United States, if you have content that targets the higher end of PPC, use twenty-five cents as an average. For the lower end, use seven cents, and if you aren't sure, use something in the middle or lower, like twelve cents. Again, these are very simplistic assumptions for this model only. You can always hope and aim for much more. For visitors from strong economies outside the United States, multiply these PPC figures by 0.7 to get 30 percent less. For visitors from developing or smaller economies—and this includes big markets where the online advertising isn't blossoming—multiply the United States PPC numbers by 0.1 to get 90 percent less. Yes, this is sad but true. On the bright side, the CTR there is usually higher.

In-text Ad Revenue Estimation—The Formula

Finally, we're getting to the actual formula. How much money can you earn from in-text ads on your website? Here's the formula: Take your net impressions, divide by 10, and multiply by the CTR to get the expected number of clicks. Then multiply the clicks by the PPC, and you have your bottom-line projected revenue. Want the eCPM? Divide the bottom-line revenue by the number of impressions and divide again by 1,000. Important: If your traffic has different geographic sources like most websites, you need to do this calculation separately according to the source and use the relative estimated PPC accordingly. This is also true if your website has different content categories. Then you have to calculate using the relevant PPC as well.

A Practical Example

Your website, www.ExampleSite.com, gets 1,000,000 page views per month, but you know that some of these visitors leave very fast. In fact, some of the pages have video only and no text, so your fill rate is about 80 percent with net impressions of 800,000. About 60 percent of your traffic comes from the United States, 10 percent comes from Canada and Germany, and the remaining 30 percent of your visitors come from India and Indonesia. Your content niche is very attractive to high-cost advertisers because it's all about financial instruments, so the PPC should be high. As for CTR, your Google AdSense ads yield about a 1 percent click-through rate.

Now we can start estimating figures for in-text ad revenue. The CTR should be about 50 percent higher, so we can assume a 1.5 percent CTR. The PPC for visitors from the United States should be high—an average of about twenty-five cents. For visitors from Canada (CA) and Germany (DE), calculate 30 percent less, so we can assume 17.5 cents. For visitors from India (IN) and Indonesia (ID), we multiply by 0.1 to get 2.5 cents.

60 percent U.S. traffic x 800,000/10 x 1.5 percent CTR x $0.25 PPC = $180 monthly revenue, $0.38 eCPM.
10 percent CA and DE traffic x 800,000/10 x 1.5 percent CTR x $0.175 PPC = $21 monthly revenue, $0.26 eCPM.
30 percent IN and ID traffic x 800,000/10 x 1.5 percent CTR x $0.025 PPC = $9 monthly revenue, $0.04 eCPM.

In total, the estimated revenue would be 180 + 21 + 9 = $210 with a general eCPM of $0.26. If your provider counted only U.S. traffic, the eCPM would have been higher ($0.38), but your bottom-line revenue would be only $180. You would also have lost 14 percent of your revenue ($30) only to see a nicer eCPM.

Why Calculate When You Can Try?

I hope that you can now do the math for your own site and estimate how much money you can earn with in-text ads. Word of caution: This formula uses generalizations and assumptions, and it disregards several parameters that can affect your revenue. It can be used for rough estimations but not much more. The best way to get an idea of how much you can earn is by simply trying it. Ask an in-text ad provider to integrate its solution with no long-term commitments, try it for a while, and get an accurate figure. A full month would give you the best projection.

Pay-Per-Click and Other Business Models— Choosing a Business Model for In-Text Ad Monetization

So let's say that you finally decided to add double-underline ads on your website. Now you need to choose which business model will work best for you. Website monetization can be managed with partners who pay for different goals. They pay per click, per acquisition, per one thousand views, per lead, and probably per anything else you can think of. For in-text ads, the best business model is pay-per-click. Remember that from the advertiser's point of view, it's cost-per-click or CPC. The justifications for this model can be found in the balance of risk.

The Balance of Risk

Advertisers are on the market to promote sales. They want to sell products or services, and even when brand awareness is all they seek, it has to eventually lead to more sales. When they pay per click, they take the entire risk of converting the clicking visitor into a customer. In other models, when they pay only for a visitor that completes another action beyond the click and turns into a lead by leaving his details or turns into a customer by buying something, part of the risk is allocated to the website publisher. True, they will pay more for a customer or a lead than for a click, but the website publisher takes the risk of visitors who are not interested in the advertisers' goods. Since the advertisers have all of the information and tools to calculate conversion rates and the probability of sales, it makes more sense that they manage this risk. The website publisher should minimize the risk and ask for payment per click.

Minimum and Fixed eCPM

Some website publishers seek a guaranteed eCPM—fixed or minimum. If it's a fixed number, and the in-text ad provider has managed to generate higher revenue, then the provider keeps the difference. If it's a minimum eCPM, the website publisher keeps the difference. In both cases, such a deal allocates more risk to the ad provider because if the ads don't yield the expected eCPM, the provider has to pay more than he got paid by the advertisers. Although this seems like a good deal from the publisher's point of view, it isn't always recommended.

Online advertising is a dynamic field with budgets that come and go. If you ask your provider to guarantee the eCPM, you actually push the provider to play it safe. This may lead to stability but only mediocre stability. Once the provider manages to get you that guaranteed eCPM, it will not try harder to surpass it. Also, if the provider is unable to keep the guaranteed eCPM, it will eventually ask to change the terms of the deal, and stability will be replaced by continuous renegotiations.

Floor PPC

Experienced publishers who know the problems of guaranteed eCPM sometimes ask for a minimal payment per click or floor PPC. The logic behind this is that if you already lose the visitor, it won't be for less than a certain sum. But this logic doesn't work when the visitor simply leaves the website by closing the browser or moving on to another website. All visitors leave at some point, and if they don't click on an in-text ad, it doesn't mean that they will click on another type of advertising.

Moreover, not all visitors have the same value. Depending on geographic location, demographic parameters, and the highlighted term of the ad, each visitor has a different value to advertisers. When you set a floor PPC, you might lose the monetization potential of certain visitors. A payment is a payment, and it's a big numbers game. Therefore, it's wise to monitor your per-click earnings and push your provider to get it as high as possible, but it isn't recommended to limit it.

Paying For Eyeballs

Some advertising campaigns seek a wide audience to build brand recognition and awareness to a certain promotion. This is very common in display ads where banners are surrounding the content and visitors are exposed to messages sometimes even for fractions of seconds. When it's eyeballs they want, advertisers mostly use the CPM model and pay for every 1,000 pairs of eyes who are exposed to the banner. With in-text ads, this isn't really relevant since in-text ads are hidden behind highlighted terms, and visitors don't see the messages before they express interest with a mouse hover. When they choose to see the message, they give much more attention than they would to an open banner, so it should be worth more. Therefore the CPM model doesn't work well for in-text ads. Clicks do!

Revenue Share is King

The most important aspect of monetizing your website's traffic with in-text advertising is the revenue share. Combined with a PPC model, this should optimize your earnings. If you trust your provider to maximize efforts and get you the best-suited advertisers, you'd better let the provider focus on professional work. The best way for you to guarantee maximum earnings is to ask for the highest possible revenue share. If you get a 60 percent revenue share deal, it means that you get 60 percent of the payment for every click. Obviously, it would be nicer to get 70 percent. Then the in-text provider will do its best to get payments for every click—the higher the better for both of you. But don't push too hard. If you somehow manage to get a 90 percent revenue share deal, your provider might lose the incentive to work hard to increase your earnings because the upside from his perspective would be too low. The bottom line is to look for the highest revenue share deal from a trusted pay-per-click provider.

Website Monetization Cycles and Seasonal eCPM Changes

After a few months with in-text ads on your website, you will probably get used to the monthly payments and accumulated revenue. At this stage, many publishers tend to think of in-text ads as a simple money machine. The integration was easy, and after some optimization these ads require no maintenance. But then the average earnings might change—either up or down—and publishers ask, "What happened?" Before rushing to conclusions, it's better to understand the industry in which in-text ad networks operate. This can shed some light on revenue fluctuations. In-text ads are not merely a money machine; they represent an entire online advertising market.

Three Market Factors

There are three main factors in the online advertising market that influence any website's monetization. The first two stem from human nature: Both your visitors and advertisers are real people with changing patterns of behavior that directly influence your earnings. The third factor is of a more mechanical nature. As smart as systems have become, the ones that manage in-text ads have some limitations that also influence the levels of your earnings. Let's review these cycles one by one.

Online Advertising Cycles

The advertisers who buy online campaigns have cycles like any other advertiser. Most prominently, advertisers are subject to seasonal increases in advertising and, of course, seasonal decreases. For example, in the United States, many advertisers spend much more around the shopping carnival that precedes the winter holidays in November and December. Many website publishers experience a surge in earnings during these months. But then comes January when they see a decline in revenue. So remember that this is a living marketplace, and when the shopping season is over many advertisers limit their campaigns. Some advertisers are linked to other types of cycles, like specific sports seasons. For example, if your website is suitable for ads related to a sport like skiing, you can expect lower revenue once the ski season is over.

Online Surfing Cycles

Just as advertisers have seasonal highs and lows, your website visitors have repeated patterns of behavior year round. In addition to the shopping or sports seasons, you probably know that your website's traffic changes with time. For example, during family-oriented holidays when people tend to spend more time with their families and less time in front of the computer, you may see a lower volume of visitors and lower revenue.

But your visitors have additional behavioral patterns that are related to your method of website monetization. If you have a community of dedicated visitors who often return to your website, you might notice a slow decrease in click-through rate (CTR) over time that will lead to lower earnings as well. The reason is obvious. Once they get used to the double-underline links, your visitors may overlook them. When this happens, you should consider if this is good for the overall user experience, or you may choose to change the link color or appearance in order to attract new attention. The human eye is very sensitive to such changes.

Automated Campaign Cycles

A third factor that influences your earnings is tightly related to the fact that the online advertising market is mostly governed by automated processes. While most systems try hard to spread budgets evenly over time, they can't measure the spending every second. If a system is set to spread the budget evenly over a whole day, it will usually divide the budgets into hourly caps. But since there are no measurements every minute, within a single hour, there may be higher spending at the beginning of the hour. Once the hourly cap is reached, there may be a drop in spending until a new hour starts.

Similarly, many systems, including Google AdWords, offer advertisers a default to set a daily budget cap. For this reason, the beginning of the day may be more profitable for websites than the last few hours of the day. This phenomenon is most visible in the monthly cycle, where earnings in the last few days of a month can be lower than the monthly average, as many campaigns simply run out of money.

Why Has Your eCPM Decreased?

When you see a decrease in your daily eCPM, don't worry. Just ask yourself whether the decrease could easily be explained by one of these cycles. Has a shopping season just ended? Could it be the end of the month? In most cases, seasonal fluctuations are self-explanatory when taking into account that in-text ads are not merely a money machine but part of the online advertising market. Waiting a few days until the beginning of a new month or season will suffice in most cases, as earnings will then go back up.

If you can't identify a relevant cycle from advertisers, visitors, or automated systems, it's time to talk with your in-text ad provider. Perhaps there's something else going on. Sometimes, an internal change or mistake requires attention. Other times, some additional optimization is needed to get back on the natural waves of highs and lows. Understanding the seasonal peaks and valleys in your earnings graphs is a first step toward knowing when it's time to act and when you simply need a little patience.

Getting Paid with in-text Ads on a Website— The Payment Threshold and the Waiting Period

Once a visitor on your website hovers over a double-underline link and clicks on an ad within the bubble, you've already earned advertising revenue. It can be as low as a few cents, but money is money, right? So why don't you get paid immediately? Well, handling payments takes effort and costs, and if you create a transaction for every cent earned, your costs will become higher than your earnings. Also, the online advertising cycle requires several offline procedures to ensure the validity of the ads served and clicking visitors, so some patience is required.

In-text ad providers—like other ad networks, including Google AdSense—set a minimum sum for payout, often called the payment threshold. As a website publisher, you get paid only after your earnings reach this number. And then, payments go out in cycles, mostly on a monthly basis, so you need to wait a little longer. In order to get paid, you first need to get to the payment threshold and then also wait for the monthly payment cycle to arrive.

Let's take an example with customary numbers: The payment threshold is $100, and the payment cycle is monthly with a waiting period of 30 days, during which the provider collects payments from advertisers and makes all necessary calculations and procedures. If, in July, you've earned $65, you're not entitled to payment because your earnings are lower than the payment threshold. This sum is, therefore, carried over to the next month. Then in August, your website yields another $80. Although this is still lower than the payment threshold, you already have a pending balance from the previous month, which brings your total to $145, entitling you to a payout. Now from the end of August you need to wait 30 days and can expect payment by the end of September.

Just to avoid a common mistake, your September earnings will not be included in the payment at the end of September but only thirty days later. Accordingly, even if you earn another $300 during September, these earnings won't be reflected until the payment at the end of October.

Payment Methods and Transaction Fees

Although most money in the world today is in the form of bits of information in various types of bank accounts which can, theoretically, travel at the speed of light, it can still prove to be quite difficult to get your website revenue from your online advertising provider. Also, some forms of payment include high transaction fees.

If both you and the provider are in the United States, the best form of payment in terms of speed, comfort, and cost, is direct deposit, also called ACH (Automated Clearing House). It is very much like a traditional wire transfer directly between bank accounts but with much lower commissions and transaction fees. In fact, the fees and commissions are close to zero. If you have a bank account in the United States, you should ask your provider to use ACH.

In some cases, ACH is limited to high-volume transfers, however. If you don't qualify for it, ask your provider if it's possible to hold your payments until you reach the minimum sum for ACH. If you can afford the wait, the minimal costs might be worth it.

International Payments

Outside the United States, the most common form of online transfers is PayPal. The advantages are transparency and safety. The disadvantages are high service commissions and severe limitations in certain countries. For small transfers, PayPal is a wise choice. If your earnings get into hundreds and thousands, you should consider alternatives to save on the commissions. Also, in some countries like Chile and Pakistan, you simply can't work with PayPal, while in other countries you can work with them but may find it very difficult to withdraw your money. In these cases, you must consider the alternatives.

In my experience, wire transfers directly between bank accounts are relevant only for big numbers because they involve a headache of details and commissions. For smaller amounts where PayPal is not available, a good alternative can be Payoneer, which sends money directly to MasterCard debit cards that are accepted worldwide, and there are other options as well. But since payment methods are not the focus here, I won't include reviews of PayPal alternatives and competitors.

Tax Forms

As it happens, all major in-text ad providers operate out of the United States and are, therefore, subject to IRS tax regulations. So to receive payments from them, the website publisher needs to fill out a form that transfers the responsibility for tax payments to the publisher. This is true even if the publisher is not located in the United States. Be sure to submit the relevant form to guarantee that your payment isn't delayed. If you don't do any business in the United States, you can replace the IRS form with a formal declaration about having no business or income in the United States.

If your in-text ad provider is located in another country, the tax requirements will be different, so take that into account.

Small Website Warning

Some blogs and websites earn only small monthly sums, but this can still accumulate into significant amounts and at least cover your costs. When choosing your provider, check the payment threshold so that your earnings won't get stuck with the provider for too long. Even more important, some in-text providers tend to discriminate against smaller publishers in the fine print. For example, the terms may state that if you haven't reached a minimum sum in a certain month, your earnings will be lost entirely. Even a bigger website may lose revenue that it rightfully produced after a slow month or if it was under construction. Make sure that you don't fall into such a trap.

Big Website Warning

When your website monetization entitles you to high payouts, you should be aware of high transaction costs. Even if you have become accustomed to PayPal, the commissions there can be significantly higher compared to ACH or wire transfers, so if you experience growth check into your choices of payment methods.

CHAPTER 7:
IN-TEXT ADVERTISING EXTRAS

Not Just Text: Video, Banners, and Display in-text Ads

In the early days of in-text advertising, the double-underline links opened bubbles with textual ads, mostly alongside a thumbnail image of the ad's landing page as a preview. With time, the text ads gave way to more and more graphic ads that looked like banners. This trend is still in progress, and the balance between text ads and banner ads is not yet fixed. In fact, this balance is very different between markets, and it seems that in markets where in-text ads are still relatively new, text ads still hold the reins, while banner-type ads are taking the lead in more mature markets.

Placing display ads within the bubbles is not a technological challenge. The bubbles can come in different sizes matching the standard banner dimensions, and running an animated banner or playing video is simply a matter of importing a different object into that location. So if it's really that simple, why aren't all in-text ads graphic, and why do they mostly start with text ads?

Ad Relevance and Noise Balance

The first aspect that makes in-text ads so attractive to publishers who respect their content is that they are subtle and don't add as much jumble as graphic banners. In an attempt to keep the noise balance in favor of the actual content, in-text ads are meant to be relatively quiet. When the bubbles themselves are filled with flashy banners, the in-text ads lose this advantage.

The second benefit of in-text ads is that they are attached to specific terms within the content, offering potential for high levels of contextual matching. When the ads are relevant, the visitors value them, and, in return, the advertisers gain real attention. This, of course, leads to higher revenue to the publishers with less annoyance to their visitors. By definition, it's easier to match text ads to specific terms than it is with banners, which tend to be less specific. While it's true that banners can be made more specific, they are not as contextual as text ads.

Why Do Display Ads Win?

In light of the ad relevance and noise balance advantages of text ads over banners, why do display ads take more and more bubble-share from in-text ads? The answer is in permission marketing and the business model. Clearly, upon an intended mouse hover, when the bubble is opened, graphic elements may attract more attention and deliver a deeper message than a few words. And it's exactly attention that advertisers seek from potential customers, aiming to achieve the gold trophy of real permission marketing. Now when advertisers buy regular display campaigns, they're counting on the banners to be placed next to the content, interfering with the visitor's interest in the content. As such, the level of expected attention is relatively low, and the price per view is also low because most visitors pay very little attention.

Banners within in-text ads are different. They are not placed and exposed unless the visitor expresses active interest in learning more about a highlighted term, and, therefore, the attention level is very high, especially when compared to a banner that is simply there surrounding the content. This permission from the visitor to get exposed to the advertisement is highly valuable to advertisers.

Then comes the business model. While text ads are mostly charged per click, the advertiser usually pays for impressions only when financing a display campaign. Clicks are just a bonus. And the price is set by the thousands of page views. The price of each such view is again low because in most of these page views, the banner will get very little attention, if any. Each view usually costs fractions of a cent. But then, if the same campaign is placed within in-text ads, each delivery receives direct, permitted attention. It's a whole different story. But while the increase in attention can be enormous, the added cost is usually not as high, and advertisers can get a very good deal.

Therefore, from the advertiser's point of view, placing display ads within in-text bubbles can prove to be very rewarding. In cases where the publisher agrees to the higher level of noise and lower levels of relevancy, the publisher also gets rewarded with higher effective revenue. Publishers also benefit from the fact that each time a visitor hovers with the mouse over an ad, the banner is displayed and counted. Therefore, publishers get paid for visitors who haven't necessarily clicked and left their website.

The Metrics Challenge

Integrating display campaigns into in-text advertising methods holds a challenge in the form of distorted metrics. Since the banners get much more attention than they would have received outside of the bubble, they also get a much higher click-through rate. When such campaigns run through widely accepted ad-serving services or marketplaces, the metrics seem to be off the standard and almost fraudulent. With time, ad servers and marketplaces learn the special characteristics of in-text ads and handle them correctly. But until this process is finalized, in-text placing is often flagged as problematic, and the provider needs to sort this out with the intermediaries.

Video in-text Ads

All of this is true for video in-text ads as well. A video played within the bubble is noisy, but it has a strong appeal and often wins over the visitor's attention. Again, there is a challenge with the metrics, and the business model may need adjustments. Still, the potential is high for both advertisers and publishers.

There's a Big Market Out There

Last but not least, display ads simply have a larger available market. While the text ads market is mostly controlled by Google, which is still outside the in-text arena, the market for display ads is more evenly shared among other ad networks that do work with in-text advertisers. This means that the big display ad market is open to in-text players and holds great potential. This big display and video market out there explains why we see—and will continue to see—more and more banners within in-text bubbles.

Not Just Bubbles: in-text Ads With Bubbles

When defining in-text ads, the little tooltip that opens upon a mouse hover nicknamed "bubble" was a fundamental part of it. But, as it usually happens with definitions, there are exceptions. Some advertising methods that insert ads dynamically within existing online content do so without the so-called bubble or with variations of it.

Generally speaking, I find the bubbles to be a crucial part of the success of in-text advertising. The ability of users to view the ad before clicking it guarantees the double permission process. When hovering with the mouse, users first ask for some more information about the highlighted term (with the double-underline), and when they click, they actually approve of seeing more of the related ad shown within the bubble. Such genuine interest in advertised content generates higher conversion rates for advertisers and, in the long run, yields higher revenue for the website publisher. Without this preview, more clicks will happen by mistake, bounce rates will be higher, and overall results for both advertisers and publishers will diminish. And yet, such bubble-less in-text ads do exist, so they're worth understanding.

Link-Only in-text Ads

Some providers offer website publishers the opportunity to integrate what seem like in-text ads that don't react to mouse hovers. Upon a click, such ads lead to the advertiser's landing page without a bubble or other form of preview. In most cases, such providers also allow the configuration of the advertising links to confusingly appear exactly like regular hyperlinks.

The obvious outcome of these link-only in-text ads is unaware clicks. Visitors to sites with such ads can't differentiate between regular or editorial links from the links that are paid for. The unavoidable result is that users become confused. They also become angry, and this anger is directed at both the website and the advertiser.

So why would anyone integrate such ads? From the publisher's point of view, misleading visitors makes sense only for websites that don't view their visitors as anything but one-time short-term revenue opportunities. Websites that don't look for returning visitors, like AdSense traps or websites that deal with traffic arbitrage, simply want clicks for immediate revenue, not much more. Some get-rich-quick programs that promote these websites may be candidates for this form of advertising.

But with this understanding, why would advertisers want to work with them? Well, there are many types of advertisers that look for volume with no focus on quality. Again, traffic arbitrage sometimes requires high volumes of clicks, and some fraudulent activities may require disguising robot clicks among genuine clicks. You can think of other examples, but they will all surely fall under dubious fields of online activity. As you can see, I personally don't like it when people are cheated or misled into clicking. Therefore I don't like link-only in-text ads.

Animated and Interactive Tooltips

There is a nicer version of bubble-less in-text ads where the regular bubble is replaced by another form of creative preview. Instead of placing the ad within a bubble-like tooltip, these in-text ads use other formats that generate the double permission process but also attract more attention. One example is a 3-D ad that pops up during a mouse hover. Another example is a big bubble that includes interactive content.

While such creative bubble replacements could prove to be very efficient, they do have a downside in the form of noise. One of the advantages of in-text ads is their subtlety, and while they hook themselves on actual content, they don't overdo it with jumping animation. This is the secret that paved the way for in-text ads to be added to reputable websites. Interactive or large animated bubbles could change the balance of content and ads, so they may not be suitable for all websites.

Added Text Link Ads / Google Text Link Ad Units

The last form of bubble-less in-text ads—at least as of this writing— comes in the form of added links. This method of advertising steps even further away from in-text advertising since it doesn't highlight existing content. Instead, it inserts additional content within the text. This can be done either by configuring text ad units within the content where ads are later added dynamically or by letting a script push the content to add textual ad units. Then these text links can perform as regular in-text ads with hovers and bubbles or as link-only text ads with no preview.

The most famous example is Google AdSense's Text Link ad units, where publishers can add a line of text links with contextually related terms that link to pages full of paid-for ads. Many website publishers integrate these ad units just above content to appear a little like a navigation bar, but this clearly confuses visitors. Others add these text link ad units between paragraphs to appear as part of the text. One should question Google's approval of these ads because they contradict Google's positive approach to online advertising. My guess is that with time, Google will back away from this format or at least restrict the integration to locations that aren't confusing.

Text link ads can be legitimate and serve visitors with added value, while creating a positive interaction opportunity for advertisers, but only when they are clearly distinguishable from the content. To Google's benefit, all text link ad units are preceded by a small headline describing them as ads. As with other issues related to contextual advertising, the clearer the distinction between editorial content and ads, the better the long-term results for all parties involved. So if you choose to use bubble-less in-text ads, keep that distinction in mind.

Not Just Ads: Informational in-text Links

These links look like in-text ads with double-underline links and a bubble that opens upon a mouse hover, but their content is different. Instead of commercial content from an advertiser, the bubble offers additional content from various sources. So they are informational links.

The links can lead to relevant pages on the same website or other websites. Sometimes, and mostly when the content is originated on another free website like Wikipedia or YouTube, the content can be made available within the bubble itself so that users won't be tempted to leave the original website. Snap, one of the pioneers of related content in-text links, focuses on the end user's experience and describes these links as a "way to give your users a more fun and interactive experience on your site or blog."

Where's the Business Model?

The initial problem with related content in-text links was the lack of a business model. True, some website publishers found that these tools increased page views through internal linking, but these dynamic links were not counted for search engine optimization (SEO), so they lost popularity. Some websites liked the idea that Wikipedia and YouTube content, which users look for anyway, was made available within their websites because it prevented them from losing visitors. But such rich content bubbles add a lot of noise to the website's design.

So, as often happens, it came down to finding a justifiable business model. Someone has to pay for the added bubbles. The problem is that website publishers hope to earn from such services running on their websites rather than pay for them, and Wikipedia and YouTube certainly won't pay for this offsite distribution.

Lacking an alternative business model, related content in-text links shifted toward regular forms of in-text advertising and started to include paid-for content within the so-called objective-related content. Services like Snap added advertising to the offered content, while in-text providers began to add non-commercial content alongside the ads within their bubbles. This way, the advertising revenue financed the free service of the related content.

A Hybrid is Born—in-text Ads Plus Related Content

Hybrid in-text links combine both seemingly objective-related information and paid-for advertising content. These links may at first appear to be a nice way to show off with added value to end users while explaining the ads as a financial must, but I find them to be highly problematic.

Again, one the most attractive aspects of in-text advertising in the eyes of advertisers is that users grant their permission to be exposed to the content. When in-text ads are mixed with informational links, visitors cannot easily identify which is which. The website's visitors then mistakenly hover over or click on ads, hoping to get non-commercial content. This mixture ultimately significantly decreases the effectiveness of in-text advertising. The more distinct the double-underline links are, the higher the conversion levels are, and the higher the CPC to the publisher and the satisfaction to the advertiser. The opposite is also true. The higher the confusion between informational links and advertising links, the lower the results for both publishers and advertisers.

Best Practices: Distinction

This analysis doesn't mean that there isn't a place for informational in-text links. Related content in-text links could add some page views and, in some cases, contribute to the overall user experience. However, to keep both visitors and advertisers happy, there should be a very clear distinction between the different types of links. If the links have the same appearance, but the shade of color is ever so slightly different, this doesn't count as a distinction. Visitors need to *clearly* understand what they're hovering over—an informational link or an in-text ad. Once they do, they will be happier and, eventually, so will advertisers and publishers.

Not Exactly Ads: in-text Ads with Search Bubbles

Have you ever hovered over an in-text double-underline link only to find a bubble that offers to search more information about the highlighted term? This is a "search bubble." When clicking on a search bubble, the visitor is led to a landing page with search results for that highlighted term. Clearly, this is not exactly an advertisement, because the visitor is only offered search results and not related content from an advertiser. But you do see quite a lot of these search bubbles among other in-text ads. Where are they coming from? And more importantly, who pays for them?

Paying for Search

Publishers do get paid per click even when the in-text bubble only contains a search link. In most cases, the advertiser is the search engine itself. In an online world dominated by Google, smaller search engines and niche search engines are forced to buy search traffic. In other words, to promote their search services, they pay for people to use them for searches.

A good example of this is Microsoft's Bing search engine. A relative newcomer with clear intentions to win market share from Google, Bing is paying for campaigns to promote searches, trying to get people to appreciate its services and come back for more searches. Other examples are business directories and specialized niche search engines, which pay for initial searches, hoping for returning users later on.

So, the in-text ad network places search bubbles, but these are actually ads paid for by the target search engine. Therefore, in the eyes of publishers, these are regular ads with a standard pay-per-click model, while in the eyes of website visitors these ads simply offer more information in the form of search results.

Paid-For Search Results

Search bubbles sometimes lead to paid-for search results. The business model here is based on the potential revenue from visitors who click on the sponsored results.

Let's clarify this with an example: Joe is looking for information about a certain disease through Google. He goes to a website with information about this disease, and one of the possible treatments is highlighted with a double-underline like an in-text ad. When Joe hovers his mouse over the double-underline, the opening bubble offers Joe the opportunity to search more information about this treatment using a health-related search engine. After he clicks, he lands on the health-related search engine's results page. These results are relevant to his search, so he's happy. He clicks on one of them from a local clinic that offers the treatment and becomes a potential customer for that clinic. The health-related search engine paid twenty cents for that click. The in-text ad network kept 30 percent of it and paid the remaining fourteen cents to the original publisher, which makes everyone happy. Now the health-related search engine specializes in health clinics and was able to sell that ad to a local clinic for seventy cents. Again, both the search engine and the clinic are happy. The clinic purchased a valid lead for a price it was willing to pay, and the search engine earned the difference between prices—fifty cents in this case.

Search bubbles are sometimes condemned for being a tool for traffic arbitrage—publishers who buy cheap traffic in the form of run-of-network (RON) campaigns and transform it into revenue from higher-paying ads. However, as shown in the example above, when handled correctly, all participants are very happy with this type of scenario. All parties earned revenue from the transaction that got the potential customer and clinic in contact. And who knows? Perhaps that in-text search bubble will help to restore Joe's health.

Shopping Comparison Bubbles

One type of in-text search bubble is purchased by shopping comparison websites. While a publisher can get paid a little more for displaying an advertisement from the final online retailer, many online shoppers prefer to go through a shopping comparison website that offers reviews of the product and price offers from different online retailers, together with reviews of the retailers themselves.

This preference has led to in-text ads with shopping comparison search bubbles. Upon a mouse hover over a double-underline link, usually of a highlighted name of a product, the opened bubble offers the visitor a shopping comparison for that specific product. The target landing page presents the visitor with shopping alternatives and reviews. Due to the nature of in-text ads that require the active permission of the visitor, shopping comparison websites find high conversion rates from such ads that bring visitors with a good chance of making a purchase.

This explains why they are willing to pay per click. Again, all sides are happy, from the publisher who got paid for the click to the network and shopping comparison website and on to the online retailer at the end of the line that gets a lead with a high potential to purchase.

Happy People

So the next time you see an in-text ad with a search box inside it from either a general search engine or a niche information provider like a shopping comparison website, you can smile. True, this is not exactly an ad, but when managed correctly by the in-text ad network, it creates a cycle of happy people.

Not Just Double-Underline:
Single, Dashed, and Other Ad Link Formats

In-text advertising comes in many formats. The original and most recognized format for these hooks—the highlighted terms that carry the ad bubble—is the double-underline. But there are other formats that could be more suitable for your website and it's important to know the differences.

I already wrote a tip relevant to this topic about using a distinct format for in-text ads. In-text ads should be subtle enough not to interrupt readers who aren't interested, but they should send a clear signal to readers about the available additional information. Using a distinct format assists your visitors in determining whether or not they're interested in the advertisers' content.

The double-underline format has been in use as a default by leading in-text ad networks and has become the industry standard over time. Readers already recognize double-underline links as standing for in-text ads, and they can make their choice: Keep on reading uninterrupted or hover with the mouse to learn more before they decide if they want to click on the advertisement. The double-underline format is not in common use for anything else, which makes it a distinct and preferred format for in-text ads.

The Evil Alternative: Single-Underline Ad Links

In the earlier days of in-text advertising, publishers offered to set the ad links with single-underlines. The justification was that readers complained that the then new double-underline links disturbed their reading. Consequently, readers clicked on ad links without knowing that they lead to advertising landing pages instead of additional non-paid-for content. I call this the "Evil Alternative" because it contradicts permission marketing. When visitors are fooled into clicking, they tend to get angry and quickly leave both the advertiser's landing page and the original website. Despite the short-run increase in click-through rate (CTR), revenue from such ad links will eventually drop as a result of advertisers refusing to work with websites that have high bounce rates. No advertiser wants to pay high pay-per-click sums for unintended clicks.

To avoid this unwanted result, the in-text ad networks had to make single-underline in-text ads require two clicks. The first click would only open the bubble without charge to the advertiser and without payment to the website's publisher. Only the second click, after the ad was opened within the bubble, would be counted for charges and payments. Although this was better than unintended clicks, the number of paid-for clicks decreased substantially with this double-click requirement, and readers found the confusion between regular links and ad links quite annoying. The bottom line is that using the single-underline format for in-text ads on a website is not recommended.

The Positive Alternative: Other Distinct Underline Formats

There is a positive alternative to the standard double-underline format, which some website publishers simply don't like. They feel it doesn't go well with their website's design or that their visitors disregard or dislike it. Publishers want to keep the best practice of using a distinct format for ad links, but they want other graphical formats. The ad networks agree. Hence the dashed, zigzag, and combined underline formats have been thrown into the online advertising ring.

Instead of the standard double-underline format, publishers can now choose other link formats that still make it clear that they're different from regular hyperlinks. Ad links can be formatted as a dashed underline, a zigzag underline, or any combination thereof. In fact, they can come in many other graphical appearances as well. As long as readers understand that they are different from regular links, these formats work quite well. It should be noted that new visitors won't recognize the in-text ads as such, since these formats are not the industry's standard that they recognize from other websites. This usually means a higher rate of hovers and clicks, which explains why this is the positive alternative. But then again, it may also annoy visitors as a new type of interruption.

Bonus: Icons Next to in-text Ads

In the spirit of searching for balance between making in-text ads stand out and not interfering with the flow of reading, there is another bonus option: Adding a small icon next to the highlighted term. Some of the leading in-text ad networks allow publishers to insert a small icon next to the ad link. This icon can be a tiny bubble symbol that signals to readers that there is a bubble waiting for them upon a hover. It can also be an icon that is relevant to the ad's content. For example, a tiny magnifying glass icon can indicate that the bubble only contains further search options. Adding such an icon may prove to be exactly what your visitors are looking for—a distinct format that helps them identify which link is a regular hyperlink and which link is a paid-for advertisement. However, some visitors find these icons to be a little too much when added to in-text ads.

Best Practices: Try and Try Again

With all of these format options for in-text ad links, the best practice is to conduct some testing. You may start with the default of double-underline links. Then, after you have accumulated enough information, test the results with other formats like the dashed underline and an icon next to the links. You should monitor both the bottom-line results and your visitors' feedback until you find the balance best suited for your website. After a while, you should probably run further testing. That's how it is with website monetization—the optimization process is ongoing. But it's also fun!

Chapter 8:

Popular Questions

Can in-text Ads Work with AdSense?

Yes, you can monetize your website with in-text ads together with Google AdSense ads. Websites integrate Google AdSense ads with almost any other kind of advertising. In fact, AdSense has become such a standard monetization tool that you can see it alongside any other method of online advertising. So why do website publishers still ask about the ability to run in-text together with AdSense? One explanation is simply that it's rather new. Another explanation may be that publishers ask about all types of ads, in-text included. Both explanations are valid.

Additionally, around the year 2006, there was an actual concern about clashes between AdSense and in-text. In Internet time, that was a long time ago, and both methods have evolved since then. But the Internet keeps a record of everything, and if you dig deep enough, you might still find warnings about this. If you do, you can relax. Anything about clashes between AdSense and in-text is old news. With a trusted in-text ad provider, you can be sure that there will be no technical clashes with AdSense ads, and, as far as I know, Google has nothing against in-text ads. In fact, it isn't unreasonable to assume that Google will probably get into the in-text ad business in the near future.

Tomer Treves

Will in-text Ads Affect AdSense Revenue?

No, in-text ads do not affect AdSense revenue. I have worked with many thousands of websites, and almost all of them integrated both Google AdSense and in-text ads. None of them reported any decrease in earnings from AdSense. It seems that the type of visitor who clicks on a banner-like ad from AdSense (these ads surround the text) is different from the type of visitor who clicks on an in-text ad within the content. They don't replace one click with the other and, therefore, have no influence on earnings. One exception to this general statement is that when in-text ads are added to an existing website, they sometimes get more attention for a short while. Then, as the double-underline links become more familiar, it goes back to normal.

How Much Revenue Can in-text Add To AdSense?

This is a tricky question since earnings from online ads differ widely depending on many different factors. I've seen websites where the in-text ad revenue was double the AdSense revenue. I've seen websites where the revenue level was approximately the same. In most cases, with a good in-text ad provider, your website revenue should not be less than half of the AdSense revenue. So you can expect your website's in-text ads to generate up to 50 percent of your AdSense revenue (on top of the AdSense earnings). Then you can hope to be surprised by even higher levels of revenue. If you get less than that, however, you should optimize your in-text ad integration. (I'll give you some tips for that later.)

Here's the promised extra insight: The best combination for website monetization through placing ads on a website is both Google AdSense and in-text ads. Accordingly, in-text ads are not an AdSense alternative but an AdSense supplement.

If you've already decided to put AdSense ads on your website, it means that you've acknowledged the fact that ads are going to interrupt your visitors' attention while they browse through your content. In fact, with the growing portion of flash banners within AdSense ads, they

76

become more and more intrusive, grabbing your visitors' attention away from the original content. If that is the case with your website—and let's face it, most websites do use AdSense—then adding in-text ads on top of AdSense is both logical and beneficial. In-text ads are not as jumpy as flash banners; they are opened only upon your visitors' active choice, and they add substantially to your revenue. It makes sense to use in-text ads together with Google AdSense.

Are in-text Ads Relevant to the Content?

I was browsing through a magazine—a real one with paper pages—and noticed a lifestyle article about a new mattress that uses three dimensions. Well, I wondered, don't most mattresses have three dimensions? But on the next page, a full-page advertisement announced a new 3-D mattress. Hmmm … Was that a coincidence? Of course, not. The magazine sold the mattress ad and probably added an editorial article about the new technology. Most magazines try to separate editorial content from advertising to keep the appearance of professional writing. Separation of paid-for ads and actual content is considered ethical. In this instance, they weren't subtle. But wait—what's wrong with relevant ads?

There seems to be a big difference between our expectations of the offline world and the online arena. While in traditional paper publications, we prefer content which is clear of advertising interests, we actually expect the ads surrounding the content on the Internet to be highly relevant to the content.

As website publishers, we insist on showing the most relevant ads, hoping that they will yield higher click-through rates and revenue. Visitors somehow accept this as supplemental to the content. Google AdSense ads are responsible for this revolution. Since the ads are placed through automated algorithms, we don't see them as affecting the editorial considerations of the publisher. Moreover, if the ads aren't relevant, we usually complain about them. And let's face it: Even though print publications try to keep ads and content separate, the ads still have to be relevant to their readership. You won't see a feminine health product ad in a men's magazine, for example.

In-text advertising is simply a form of contextual advertising. So, of course, in-text ads are relevant to your content. But since there are examples where they are less relevant, this question calls for some further discussion.

One of the publishers I've been working with has integrated in-text ads for the first time. During the first month, he served ads to no less than 20 million unique visitors. When summarizing the first month's results, the publisher was generally very happy with the revenue and feedback, but he highlighted one e-mail from a frequent visitor who complained about an ad that was not relevant. My first response to the complaint was, "Great, this is good news!" How come? Simple. It's true that an irrelevant ad isn't a good user experience, but if you get just one complaint out of 20 million visitors, you have a very good success ratio. There are no guarantees that any contextual advertising technology will be perfect. There's nothing like a bullet-proof method with perfect relevance, not even with Google AdSense, so as long as the vast majority of ads are relevant, that's good enough.

And is it really not relevant? in-text ads can be less relevant when the content isn't focused. Any contextual algorithm, as smart as it may be, will have problems with pages that contain a mix of issues. In such cases, the ad should at least be relevant to the hook—the highlighted term.

Another factor that can reduce relevancy is geography. When the visitor comes from a country with less online advertising, it can be difficult to match the ads with high relevancy. To improve this, make sure that your in-text ad provider has enough advertising coverage in the countries of your most important visitors, and be tolerant to less relevant ads in other regions.

Last but not least, relevancy is in the eye of the advertiser. While you may think that an ad is not relevant, take into consideration that the advertiser has specifically chosen to match the ad to the term and context in question. A professional in-text ad provider only places ads with direct response to advertising campaigns that target context and terms. For example, if the chosen term is "London Hotel," you'd probably expect a travel ad. But then, if you see an ad for a T-shirt website, don't be alarmed. It could be that this T-shirt website is now selling new Madonna merchandise, and Madonna is on her way to a big concert in London. Hence, the advertiser is targeting tourists who are heading to London for the show.

Are Your Hooks Relevant?

In addition to measuring the relevancy of the ads to the content, another important factor is the relevancy of the highlighted terms to the content. Before a visitor hovers over an ad, the visitor shows interest in links which are relevant to the content. When the highlighted terms are relevant, you should see higher rates of hovers. Matching the ads themselves comes next. So first, ask yourself this: Are the terms relevant? This should be a good start.

You Can Improve in-text Ad Relevancy

If you still feel that the in-text ads on your website are not relevant enough, consider the following options. First, calculate the seriousness of this issue. If you're thinking about just a few ads out of thousands, it's probably not a serious problem. Second, consider the context and the geography. The more focused the content and the bigger the market for online advertising in this country, the higher the relevancy should be. If the market is not that big and the content is not very focused, achieving high relevancy will be difficult. Third, look at it from the advertiser's point of view. He thinks the ad is relevant, so try to understand why.

If, after considering these options, you still feel that the ads are not relevant, it's time to contact your in-text ad provider. There's much you can do together to improve the situation. Your provider can work with you to improve the algorithm and customize it to your website, direct specific advertisers to your website, and assist you with monitoring and analyzing results. After all, it's contextual advertising.

Can a Big Website Monetize with in-text Ads?

In-text advertising started as a monetization solution for smaller websites and blogs, but over time more and more big reputable websites added in-text ads to their monetizing plans. So, yet, in-text ads work well for the big guys. They serve as an AdSense supplement and add 30 percent to 60 percent on top of AdSense earnings, so this is a big incentive to give in-text ads a chance.

I recently had the opportunity and privilege to work closely with several large websites, including Squidoo.com and Britannica.com. What follows are a few insights as to how to best integrate in-text ads into big websites.

The major, or perhaps even the only, characteristic that all big websites share is their volume of traffic. In fact, this is probably the definition of a big website: A website that gets lots of visitors. Accordingly, the first concern that a publisher of a big website should consider is the robustness of the solution selected for monetization.

There are more than twenty in-text ad providers, and with the expansion of in-text penetration this number keeps growing. However, many of these providers are making their first steps in the field, and such new systems may not always be able to support large volumes of visitors. The limitations can be in the automatic realm. Is the IT infrastructure capable of withholding millions of queries and clicks every hour? The established in-text providers have proven that yes, it's more than possible. So just make sure that you're working with one of those.

Another limitation is the manual aspect of integration. Some in-text providers require manual involvement in the choice of highlighted terms and the matching of ads to text. For a website with a high volume of content or with dynamic content, manual involvement in the process is inefficient, so you need to check this with the potential provider as well.

Lots of Content and Ajax

Some of the larger websites also tend to have a lot of content on each page. The in-text algorithm needs to analyze the text in real time without delaying the loading time. Some in-text providers solve this by caching the content and doing the analysis offline, but since the online advertising market is rapidly changing, offline analysis may cause you to lose monetization potential. Therefore, a big publisher should make sure that the content analysis is done online with each page's loading but with no delays in the website's behavior.

If each web page has a large volume of content, such as an encyclopedia, the publisher may consider using Ajax for loading the content only when users scroll down. In such cases, the in-text algorithm needs to run again and again with each scroll. Otherwise the monetization will be limited to the first few paragraphs only. Britannica uses Ajax with in-text ads perfectly. If you have a large volume of content, make sure that the in-text ad provider can manage it professionally and maximize your potential earnings.

Multiple-Level Reporting

Big websites also tend to cover different types of content. A website can have an articles area and a forum, for example, or a portal can have both local news and sports news. Squidoo, for example, has both regular articles and a specialized section for books. If you take your website monetization seriously, you should probably monitor the results of each section separately, like with Google AdSense channels. In-text ads are no different, and you should ask your in-text ad provider to supply you with multiple-level reporting.

The larger in-text advertising providers work with website networks as well and should be able to provide both aggregated reports and separate reports for each site. Such reporting systems can easily be used for monitoring different sections of a big website.

Niche Content and Advertisers

You can imagine that it's easier to sell ads for a website focused on new family car models than a general web portal. Bigger websites often have many categories of content and varied demographics, so this means that the in-text ad provider needs to be able to match wide-category advertisers or multiple-niche advertisers. Some in-text ad providers focus on specific areas and have difficulties matching ads for big websites with a wide variety of content. If you have such a site, make sure you get the service that you need.

The Internet is open to all, and don't we just love it that way? But it brings a challenge to monetization, especially for bigger websites. At least 20 percent of visitors to most websites come from outside of the site's main market, and that percentage can be much higher for some websites. For big websites, these foreign visitors can accumulate to vast numbers, and there's no reason that they won't also be treated as customers.

Clearly, since the online advertising arena can be different in each country, serving in-text ads in many markets can be difficult, but it's possible. In fact, visitors from some seemingly unlikely countries often prove to have a higher click-through rate. This calls for further research, but the explanation probably comes from different surfing cultures and fewer offline advertising attacks. When you integrate in-text ads into a big website, you should ask about international traffic, and your provider should be able to monetize it as well.

Contract Changes and Higher Revenue Share

When joining online services, in-text advertising included, you are required to accept the standard terms and conditions. For big publishers, entering into legal contracts usually involves going through the legal department, which always wants to contribute its wisdom to the contract. While this will surely slow down the process, it makes sense, so don't forget this step in the integration process. You can sign up online and then negotiate an addendum to the agreement.

One major change you should consider does not require legal involvement. A big website can leverage the large online ad inventory to request a higher revenue share. From my experience, this can add up to very high numbers, but don't push your provider too much. You want the provider to be happy too or the incentive to get you higher revenue will be diminished.

Your Very Own Customized Bubble

Each in-text ad provider utilizes its own design for bubbles, but this appearance can be customized. Since this does take some work, integrating a customized bubble is mostly relevant to big websites. If you're lucky to be included in this group, you should consider asking for your very own bubble, matching it to your site's overall look and feel and perhaps promoting your brand as you go.

Testing / Trial Period with in-text Ads

So are you now seriously considering to monetize your mega website with in-text ads? Even if you've checked all relevant issues to make sure you've found the right solution for you, don't you want to test it first? Integrating in-text ads into a website takes very little technical effort so testing isn't difficult. Starting with a one-month trial period sounds like a step in the right direction, especially for a big website. My guess is that after some optimization and successful testing, you will stay for the long haul.

Do in-text Ads Work on iPhones and Mobile Devices?

The combination of in-text advertising and the mobile web holds great potential for advertisers. The combination of actual permission from potential customers to view an advertisement that is related to a specific term, together with the location and additional information from the mobile network, can yield high conversion rates for advertisers—especially local advertisers. This combination also promises publishers high revenue from their websites, but some changes are still required.

It isn't news that the web is going mobile, but when the method of access changes, other things are affected as well. Only time will tell how the user experience will be modified. Currently, the dominating format of access to the Internet through mobile devices is either by touch screens or tiny displays. In both cases, there's no mouse or cursor.

Since in-text ads require a mouse hover from the user, the lack of a mouse requires another trigger to open advertising bubbles. The aggressive option is to use in-text links without bubbles so that users who touch the double-underline links will be redirected to the advertiser's landing page without reading the initial ad. While this will drive click-through rates up, it will decrease the quality of visitors and the overall results.

I hear this question again and again: Do in-text ads work through the iPhone? The short answer is yes, they do. The longer answer is that yes, they do, *but* the in-text ad networks still need to improve the interface, enlarging the closing button on the bubble and requiring two clicks from users or one of the alternative modes discussed in this chapter. This is, of course, also true for other mobile devices like Google's Nexus One. It can work on mobile devices without a touch screen as well but to a lesser extent.

The Two-Clicks Mode and Alternatives

The more reasonable alternative, as mentioned above, is to require two clicks. The first click or touch on the screen would only open the bubble with the ad inside. Then the user would have two options—either closing the bubble and remaining on the original page or touching the bubble and continuing to the advertiser's landing page. To enable this choice, the closing button or "x" mark should be enlarged for easy access with bulky fingers. Under this double-click mode, advertisers would be very happy because users would grant active permission twice to get to their landing pages. So the advertisers won't have to pay for unintended clicks.

The problem with the double-click mode, however, is that it will decrease the click-through rate, and publishers will see a much lower volume of clicks. To compensate the publishers for the loss of clicks, advertisers will probably need to pay higher prices per click (PPC), but with the conversion potential this should be worthwhile for them.

There are two other viable possibilities. The first is to charge advertisers for the display of the bubble even without the click, which should work well for branding campaigns. Such displays are better than standard mobile ads because they're triggered only upon the user's interest, and attention is guaranteed. The second possibility is to open the bubble upon the first click, display the ad, and redirect the user to the advertiser's landing page after a couple of seconds. This mode is aggressive, but with the permission of both publisher and advertiser it can work well for certain campaigns. To avoid visitor frustration, it would be best to use this mode when the landing page offers genuine added value like freebies or highly relevant search results to the visitor.

In-text Ads and the iPad

Assuming that Apple's iPad will be as successful as expected, the in-text ad networks will also need to make the required adjustments to be sure that their ads work on it properly. My best guess is that it will be similar to the iPhone, and the same changes will take place.

In-text Ads and the Kindle

I haven't seen in-text ads on Amazon's Kindle, but the market of digital books is boiling. So it's logical to assume that some digital readers will offer free books in return for exposure to advertising. Here too in-text advertising has tremendous potential. You can imagine that when reading Alex Garland's *The Beach*, right next to the beautiful description of the Thai island and highlighting the beach's name, there will be an in-text ad with an offer for a vacation in Thailand. This could do magic for both readers and advertisers. Technically, it's possible to integrate in-text ads to run on digital books, and the near future will probably include this combination as well. See you in Thailand!

Do in-text Ads Work with Spanish Content?

Surprisingly, online publishers often ask if they can monetize their websites with in-text ads even if their content isn't in English. The answer is that, of course, you can. The question sounds surprising because most monetization schemes, including Google AdSense and other AdSense alternatives, do work in many languages. But it's a very legitimate question. In-text ads are closely tied to the actual text, so the provider needs to be able to analyze content in each supported language. And, as it turns out, not all providers can support languages other than English. So the first part of the answer is yes, but you must check with the provider to see if your language is supported.

The second part of the answer is that you must also consider the geographic aspect. Even if an in-text ad provider supports a language, the provider must also support the geographic location of the visitors. For example, let's say that a provider supports monetization of German content. It's a good start. But if this provider only has ads for the

American market, visitors from other German-speaking countries will be left untouched. If, for some reason, you target German-speaking visitors from the United States, it may work. But if you're counting on visitors from Germany and Austria, U.S. ads won't be enough. Accordingly, before choosing your in-text ad provider, make sure that there's both support for your website's language and for your visitors' major locations.

More and more websites today offer content in multiple languages. This is true in countries like Canada, where both English and French are required, and in the United States, where Spanish works well next to English. But it's also common in international websites that operate in many different languages. If a big website has content in English, German, Spanish, and French, there's no reason to integrate in-text ads on the English section only. Working with one provider to cover all languages will leverage the website's reach to get better monetization results.

Usually, a question like this comes with a follow-up question: Can I see some examples? Clearly, English examples for in-text are everywhere, and I always like to point out Britannica and Squidoo. If you're interested in other languages, I can direct you to a couple of examples from my own experience. For an example of in-text ads on a Spanish website, see PuntoFape.com, and for an example of in-text ads on a French website, see Top-Serie.org. If you need more, drop me a line—in any language!

Can Readers Opt Out from or Remove in-text Ads?

Sometimes, despite their subtlety and clear advantages for the website's publisher, visitors complain about the introduction of in-text ads to a website. Most often, this happens when a website has a community of regular visitors who are not always open to changes. From my experience, the number of complaints will be very low when compared to the total number of visitors, and the complaints will stop after a short while. Nonetheless, sometimes a publisher must deal with complaints. This is especially true when the complaining visitor is an important member of the community or simply a noisy one.

Before the Complaints, Be Transparent and Explain

The best way to respond to complaints about in-text ads is to avoid them entirely by being transparent and explaining to your visitors why you are adding the ads to your website. Share with your readers that you need advertising revenue to cover your costs and keep the content free. It will build a stronger relationship with them. If you highlight the advantages of in-text ads, you will most likely avoid all complaints. Your in-text ad network should have a ready-made paragraph that can help you draft your explanation.

The best place for an explanation is in a blog post or your FAQ section. If you have a dynamic content website or blog, a link to the explanation from a sidebar will maintain transparency and gain appreciation from your readers.

If complaints persist, you can offer your visitors the choice of actively removing in-text ads. Theoretically, this will lower your potential revenue because these visitors won't click on the ads, but a visitor who complains is unlikely to click anyway.

So, how can users remove in-text ads? Your in-text ad network should be able to provide you with a link that will enable visitors to opt out. This link usually leads to an explanation about the ads and where visitors can choose to remove them. Technically, these visitors pick up a cookie on their computers that tells the in-text script to refrain from highlighting links for them.

Having this option may also be helpful when you want to persuade your team to accept this new type of ad for your websites.

Smart Ad Placement for Returning Users

Some websites have a core community of frequent users and choose not to show them in-text ads when they return to a site. These returning users can be an important part of the website's goals, but in some cases they simply don't click on ads. Still, they do become annoyed by the ads. If you have users like this, you probably know them already. They can be identified by how they reach your website—by direct approach as opposed to Google search, for example, or through logging in as registered users.

If you know that your core community of visitors generates much less per-per-click (PPC) advertising revenue because they simply don't click on ads, it might be wise to remove PPC ads from their user experience entirely. (You would still be able to gain some revenue by display ads that pay per impression.)

How can you remove in-text ads for your website's returning visitors? First, you need a method to identify them—a cookie, sign-in, or approach link. Then in your design, have the in-text script run only on pages that are loaded for other users. If the balance of new and returning users in your case is relevant, you can also focus on the other group. For example, you can identify the visitors who arrive to your website through Google and other search engines and have the script run only for them.

Please note, of course, that this will lower your revenue, and you should take this into consideration before removing in-text ads for entire groups of users. In the overall balance of your website, however, it could be a way of avoiding complaints from regular users, while still monetizing other sources of traffic to your website.

In-text Ads—Any Objections?

I hope your new line of thinking is something in this spirit: "Okay, I'm convinced. I understand the advantages and I want to tap into this hidden treasure. I want in-text ads on my site. But … You know, there are so many hurdles to jump over, so many people objecting to the idea—my visitors and community members, the authors and editors, the website's designer and the IT team, even my boss … I need some answers." Well, here they come.

Community Members Have Something to Say

You will probably receive complaints from visitors and community members, such as: "Dear Webmaster, Why do I see double-underline links? What's with the new in-text ads? I loved your website the way it was before!"

For such cases, here's a potential response: "Dear Visitor, Thank you for the compliment and for reading my website. As you well know, creating all this content and keeping the website up for you and the other readers and community members take a lot of effort and money. To finance this operation, I had to put ads on my website. This way, you can enjoy it all for free. The new double-underline links are in-text ads. They bring you relevant content from advertisers and when you click on an ad, they pay me a few cents. As opposed to the banners we already have that might disturb you a little when you're reading, these new links are only there if you're truly interested. They will only open a bubble with a small advertisement once you hover with your mouse over them. If you're not interested, you can simply continue reading without interference. I'm sure you can understand this and I look forward to receiving more feedback. Thanks!"

By the way, you won't necessarily get objections from readers and community members. Many of them already know what in-text ads are and they got used to them in other websites. Even if you do get a complaint, don't get alarmed. In most cases, you will get just a few complaints out of many visitors, which means that all the others approve the new method. And also, within just a few days the complaints will fade away. It is also recommended to add a clause or an FAQ explaining what in-text ads are and why you need them. In rare cases when the community of regular visitors still objects, you can offer them the option to opt out of the in-text ads and click on a button that switches them off.

Authors and Editors Never Like Ads

You might also receive complaints from writers, such as: "Dear Editor in Chief: I don't like the new double-underline links because they ride on top of my prestigious original content that I write for you. This is humiliating!"

Here's a potential response: "Dear Writer: I really liked your recent post—well done! As you know, in order for me to keep paying you and finance our wonderful online project, we need money. The revenue from the banners is not enough anymore, so we had to insert new methods of website monetization. These double-underline links supplement your content with relevant advertising, but they don't interfere with continuous reading or alter your content in any way. In fact, while animated banners try to grab the attention of your readers away from your content, these new links are optional, and the ads don't open up unless the readers hover over them intentionally. Some of the banners that Google AdSense places these days include much more disrespectful messages. The in-text ads are subtle and relevant. Please, let's give them a try, and I'm sure that with time you will learn to love them and prefer them to other ads. You wouldn't want me to insert full-page ads that cover your content entirely, right?!"

Web Designers Want Control

You might also get a complaint from a web designer: "Dear Website Owner: I'm responsible for the design of this beautiful website, and I don't remember including double-underline links on it!"

Here's how you might respond: "Dear Designer: I love the website's design, and so do all of our visitors. You're brilliant! The new double-underline links are, in fact, in-text ads. They help me make additional money from the website so that I can pay for your beautiful work. Because the in-text ads don't take any space on the website, they actually leave you more freedom to design the website as you like. You can also determine the color of the links and easily control their general appearance to match your design. When these in-text ads earn us enough money, we will be able to remove some of the display banners. Then you'll have the liberty to add more white spaces, which are the latest fashion in online design. With the new revenue from in-text ads, I can now even pay you on time!"

The IT Team Hates More Work

Then of course there's the IT team. They'll no doubt have something to say about it too: "Dear Publisher: We have enough work already maintaining your IT infrastructure and keeping your website up at all times with the recent surge in traffic. We don't have time to integrate in-text ads as well. Sorry."

So what can you say to that? "Dear IT Team: Thank you for all your efforts. We broke a record in traffic yesterday, and the website is performing remarkably. However, we had to insert the new in-text ads to help finance the operation. The good news is that this shouldn't take you more than a minute. All you have to do is take this one line of JavaScript and add it to the footer of the template page just before the Google Analytics script. Everything else is automated from the loading through the text analysis and keyword highlighting, and on to the hovers, clicks, and payments. The new script won't affect the IT work on the website at all. Can you please devote one minute to this? It will pay off quickly."

Your Boss Loathes Changes

But what if your boss complains? "Dear Subordinate: Stop hassling me with all of your ingenuity and changes. I've been in the publishing business for sixty-eight years now, and I like it as it is. We had enough changes already."

You might say: "Dear Boss: You taught me that money talks, right? Well, here's a new source for additional revenue that can add more on top of all of our other advertising earnings. In-text ads can be a significant source of income. *Encyclopaedia Britannica* has been in the publishing business for 150 years, and it's using them. Even your marketing guru, Seth Godin, has added them on his brilliant website, Squidoo. We don't have to commit to anything. We can start with a trial for a couple of weeks, see how much it pays, and decide at that time. I've already convinced the designer and the IT team. I think it's really worth a try, and I can handle it all by myself."

By the way, if you need examples from your specific field, drop me an e-mail, and I'll send them to you.

From Absence through Protest to Legitimacy— The Advertising Penetration Cycle

I have told you about the cycle that every new advertising method goes through. It begins with early adopters, is followed shortly by early objectors, and then settles right in the middle of the mainstream. In-text ads are no different, and they're already past the objections and en route to becoming an industry standard. Once you're personally convinced about the benefits of in-text ads, all you have to do is climb over these obstacles from your community, editors, designers, IT team, and boss.

Advertising Campaigns with in-text Ads

But what about all of this from the advertiser's point of view? The advertiser's fantasy has always been a medium where highly targeted potential customers seek specific information and knowingly choose to be exposed to ads. Sponsored search ads fulfilled this fantasy. When people search online, they are looking for specific information, and their location and some other characteristics are known. They're also willing to click on search results, including sponsored ads. This explains the phenomenal success of Google AdWords for both advertisers and Google.

In the online world, display ads, mostly in the form of banners, represent the opposite end. Much more like traditional media, banners need to interrupt potential customers while they're doing something else. Like TV ads, they ask potential customers to stop reading the content they're enjoying and, instead, pay attention to paid-for messages. This is why advertisers need the vast exposure of banner ads to get results. So we price display advertising by the thousands.

From the advertiser's point of view, in-text advertising is much closer to search ads than to display ads. While people are asked to pay attention when they're doing something else (mostly reading), they aren't actively interrupted like with jumpy banners. This explains why in-text ads come very close to advertisers' fantasies about permission marketing.

What to Expect: CTR, Bounce Rates, and Conversion

The engagement of potential customers with ads that they have knowingly chosen to view leads to relatively high conversion rates. Clearly, conversion depends on many factors, and there isn't a specific number that can be projected for all ads and products. You can expect higher conversion rates than with display ads, however, and results that are closer on the spectrum to search ads. True, the conversion rate will not be as high as with search ads, but the cost per click could be significantly lower and the click-through rate higher. So the overall results should get very close.

In-text ads yield more clicks, which advocates say is due to smart algorithms that highlight the most relevant terms. While this is true, it's also true that in-text ads still attract more attention because they're relatively new. With the growing penetration of this new method of advertising, the initial interest in the new format will decline. Then the genuine interest in the advertiser's message will remain to justify the click rate, which will probably be a little lower but still much higher than with display ads.

An unfortunate side effect of the high click-through rate that stems from interest in the format itself, as opposed to the interest in the ad's content, is a higher bounce rate. As an advertiser, you should expect more visitors that leave your landing page quickly. These visitors were probably mostly interested in seeing how this new type of ad works. While this behavior should decline with time, it still affects your results negatively, so you should anticipate it and include it in your calculations. Still, despite the higher bounce rate, the genuine interest of most visitors and the relatively low click costs will yield high conversion rates.

Tips to Improve Online Advertising Results

When you first launch an advertising campaign with in-text ads, please do your homework. Simply copying your AdWords campaign will work, but it won't maximize your potential results. One major difference is the keyword format. While you try to target what people are searching for when including sponsored search results, in-text hooks—those double-underline links—are part of the written text. Think about that when you do your keyword research.

Also, keep in mind that the in-text bubble is limited to a single ad. There are formats that allow more ads, but the limited space and attention lead to one ad per hover de facto. This means that you can't set your CPC to aim for mid-level or lower-end results. Since only one ad will be placed, your CPC calculations should aim at the first place. Among other things, try adding just a little to your CPC, as an ad with eleven cents usually stands a better chance than an ad with a round price of ten cents.

Due to the temporary issue with higher bounce rates, keep your landing pages as clear as possible. This way, visitors who are new to the in-text format won't be confused. Help them easily identify your call to action. This tip is clearly relevant to all online advertising, but it's more important with new advertising methods.

For the last tip to improve your advertising with in-text ads, I must first apologize. I'm going to recommend working with direct in-text providers, but I also work for one of those. So you can disregard this tip, or you can consider it for the reasons that follow. I work with most textual CPC marketplaces, and those ad networks are doing an amazing job at getting potential customers and advertisers together. It's true that they take their share of the CPC, and you could bypass them. I think they bring real value to the table, however. Still, that isn't the reason that I recommend working directly with the in-text providers. The ad networks' systems were created to place ads next to search results or within websites like AdSense does; in both cases several ads are served each time. Their pricing mechanisms and other technical filters make it difficult to maximize results from in-text ads. For the time being, therefore, I recommend that advertisers try working directly with in-text providers. I also recommend that the ad networks improve their compatibility with in-text advertising so that everybody can be happy.

Green Search: Planting Real Trees with a Click

Most of us use Google every day. Multiple times. Most of us are also aware of the issue of climate change. In fact, our own usage of computers—and even Google—contributes a little to climate deterioration. But there is an alternative search option that gives back to Earth.

MyGoodPage.com is a Google-based search engine that utilizes revenue from advertisers to "do good," as they call it, and right now it's focused on planting trees. From the user's point of view, the website looks very much like Google, and since it's powered by Google the search results are the same as Google.

What's the difference? As with Google search, there are some sponsored results from advertisers who are charged per click. In the case of a regular search with Google, all advertising revenue goes directly to Google. When using MyGoodPage.com, Google generously shares a portion of the advertising revenue with MyGoodPage.com, and these funds are directed toward planting trees.

In February 2010, the Civis Mundi organization carried out the first planting expedition financed by MyGoodPage.com. As you can see in a video posted on the MyGoodPage.com blog, not only did participants plant beautiful trees, but this expedition also involved educational activities for local children in southern Brazil, helping them to learn to appreciate nature and become young ambassadors for forest preservation.

Many people already use MyGoodPage.com today as their homepage, and the website is ranked by Alexa as one of the top 150,000 sites in the world. You can also spread the word about this project by posting about it on your blog, Facebook page, or Twitter.

Disclosure: in-text Ads That Plant Trees

Infolinks and I are highly involved with the MyGoodPage.com project. Instead of just donating money, Infolinks engaged its network of website publishers in this social responsibility project by donating in-text advertising campaigns to raise awareness about MyGoodPage. com and to draw direct potential green searchers to the website.

CHAPTER 9:
CONCLUSIONS AND THE $1,000 COUPON

Most websites have a hidden treasure within them that is yet to be monetized. The option of receiving an additional stream of revenue with effective CPM that's measured in whole dollars, not cents, without sacrificing any space on your website simply cannot be ignored. In-text advertising is a rising method of online advertising and of website monetization which deserves serious consideration.

Websites like Squidoo and Britannica already monetize with in-text ads, earning effective CPM measured in whole dollars, not cents. So it's time to reconsider in-text advertising.

When contextual ads first appeared and were placed on early adopters' websites, they were frowned upon. The delicate borders between editorial content and advertising were at stake. Several years later, Google AdSense seems to be an integral part of almost every website where the publisher seeks to keep good content available for free. Just like any advertising method before it, contextual ads have gone through the typical cycle: from absence through protest to legitimacy. In-text ads are now going through the same cycle and are on the verge of becoming standard practice.

The leading in-text advertising networks now rank high on all relevant lists, and together they cover billions of page views and many millions of dollars. This niche business has gone mainstream.

The secret to the success of in-text ads is found in what Seth Godin coined a decade ago as "permission marketing." in-text ads fulfill the visionary circumstances in which potential customers willingly choose to be exposed to advertising messages. As such, they yield high returns on advertising campaign investments and offer website publishers a strong monetization opportunity.

Typically, advertisers are on a quest to win over the attention of potential customers, but in a noisy world this task has become very difficult. In the online realm, advertisers have turned up the level of interruptions to get the same level of attention. As a result, advertising units have become louder and louder with flash animation, video, and sound, taking over large parts of websites and disturbing the balance of good content vs. advertising.

With in-text ads, visitors to a website are not interrupted. There are no animated banners or video characters that walk across the screen. The double-underline links merely signal to readers that there's more, but the ad doesn't show up without permission. When an interested reader actively hovers over a double-underline link, he independently decides to be exposed to an advertisement. And there is no charge to the advertiser yet. If the permission stops there, the reader can move the mouse away, the bubble will disappear, and he can go on reading. Only if the reader is interested in the ad placed within the opened bubble and clicks on it will he be redirected to the advertiser's landing page, at which time a charge to the advertiser will be made. At this point, the website publisher also gets paid.

This double-action process means that the potential customer has given his permission *twice* to be exposed to the advertiser's content. Advertisers find that such visitors are good candidates for their messages, and publishers find that their readers are much less frustrated with these types of ads.

In the last two years, online advertising and monetization experts have seen in-text ads become a means for bloggers to cover their costs, but these ads have also been placed on fantastic websites like Squidoo. Furthermore, despite some initial concerns, well-established brands have incorporated in-text ads in their business models, including traditional publishers like *Encyclopaedia Britannica*. Remarkably, in-text ads are now served to an estimated 500 million unique users every month, and this number is growing rapidly.

So why don't all websites tap into this hidden treasure? Well, it won't be long before most will join the party. Integrating in-text ads into a website takes about one minute and requires a simple copy-paste of a short JavaScript. Within a single day, the publisher earns revenue, which can be significant and much higher than some very popular display ads. To make the introduction of the new ads easier, publishers can offer their visitors the opportunity to opt out of in-text ads, and publishers can also control the number of links, as well as their graphic appearance.

The online publishing business is mostly an ongoing struggle of providing good content, which has real costs, while keeping it available for free. We don't put ads on our websites for their beauty; we use them to finance the operation and keep our visitors happy with free information. In-text ads are subtle and are less noisy than the other ad formats that are frequently used. They can add a new source of revenue on top of other types of advertising and are certainly worth a try. Do you remember the time when you considered adding Google AdSense or an equivalent program to your website? It's time to give the same consideration to in-text ads, or you really are missing out on a hidden treasure.

The $1,000 Coupon

This book is called *The Hidden Treasure in Your Website*, but there's an additional small treasure within the book itself. As promised, there's a coupon—a big one. I collected the materials and experience for writing this book during my first two years of working for Infolinks, one of the top in-text advertising networks, where I had the pleasure of leading the business team. Clearly, the Infolinks team is happy to see this book published because it promotes in-text ad monetization, so that's how we managed to include the coupon here.

If you follow the advice in this book to uncover the hidden treasure in your website by integrating in-text ads, Infolinks will double your first month's earnings up to $1,000 with this coupon. Not bad for a start, right?

What's the catch? Well, all coupons have fine print detailing terms and conditions, and so does this one. First, your website must be approved by the Infolinks team and must abide by their terms and conditions. Second, you can only use the coupon once per publisher, and it's only good for new publishers with Infolinks. Third, the coupon is valid through the end of December 2011. While Infolinks reserves the right to extend the validity period, it also reserves the right to shorten the validity period or change its terms at any time.

There is also a business catch. Not all websites will receive $1,000 from Infolinks. If you've read the chapters about potential revenue, you know by now that not all websites will earn $1,000 in their first month with in-text ads. Depending on your volume of traffic, type of content, and geographic focus, you can earn anything from $1 to $1 million. Using this coupon, Infolinks will double your first month's earnings by *up to* $1,000, so if you earn $100, you will get an extra $100 for a total of $200. If your earnings are $4,000, you will get an extra $1,000 for a total of $5,000. Still not bad, right?

To use the coupon, during your initial sign-up with Infolinks you need to enter the following text in the "Comment" field: "Coupon: Hidden Treasure." It's quite simple, but please note that you must do this during your initial sign-up. Otherwise, it will be very difficult for the system to identify the coupon.

So what are you waiting for?

Contact Me

I look forward to continuing this discussion with you. I invite you to read updates, join the discussion, and contact me through my blog at http://OnlineSiesta.com.

About the Author

Tomer Treves is the chief marketing officer of Infolinks, an ad network that specializes in contextual in-text advertising (www.infolinks.com). He also writes a blog about in-text ads at OnlineSiesta.com.

Index

A

ACH (Automated Clearing House), 57, 59
AdBrite, 39–40
Adult-oriented content, 40–41, 45
Advertising. *See* Online advertising
Affiliate programs, 13, 16
Affinity, 39–40
Ajax, 81

B

Back button, 32–33
Bing, 69
Bounce rate, 95
Britannica, 80, 81, 87, 93, 98, 99
Browsers, 33–37
Bubbles, 12, 60–64, 68–71, 83
Business models, 11, 50, 61–62, 67, 69–70

C

Chitika, 39–40
Chrome, 33–34, 37
Clicksor, 40
Click-through rate (CTR), 15, 47, 94–95
Color, 26–27, 55
Content analysis, 81

Conversion rates, 94–95
Cost-per-click (CPC), 34, 47
Coupon, 100–101

D

Dashed underline format, 73
Digital books, 86
Direct deposit, 57
Double-underline format, 10–11, 23–26, 71–72

E

Earnings. *See* Revenue
Effective cost-per-mille (eCPM)
    described, 43–44
    automated processes and, 21
    decrease in, 55–56
    Internet Explorer and, 35
    minimum and fixed, 51
    optimizing of in-text ads, 15

F

Fill rate, 34, 44–45
Firefox, 33–34, 36–37
Foreign language providers, 41, 86–87

G

Geo-filtering, 45
Godin, Seth, 6, 17, 93, 98
Google
  Gmail, 4–5
  MyGoodPage.com, 96–97
  Nexus One, 84
Google AdSense
  amount of income and, 16, 76
  channels, 81
  click-through-rate (CTR) and,
    47
  as contextual ad, 9, 77
  foreign languages and, 86
  integrating with in-text ads,
    75–77
  nonintrusiveness of, 2
  payment threshold and, 56
  publisher's point of view and, 8
  Text Link ad units and, 65–66
  two click requirement of, 16
Google AdWords, 55, 94
Google Analytics, 20, 44

H

Hooks, 10, 28, 78, 79
Hybrid in-text links, 67–68

I

Infolinks, ix, 38–39, 41, 97, 100–
  101
Informational in-text links, 66–68
International traffic, 41, 45–46, 48,
  78, 82, 86–87
Internet Explorer, 33–34, 35–36
Interruption advertising, 6–7, 94, 99

In-text ads
  described, vii–viii, 3–4, 9

advertisers approval of, 14, 18,
  93–94
alternative formats for, 71–74
with animated and interactive
  tooltips, 65
banners within, 61–62, 63
bubble *vs.* pop-up, 12
color of links, 26–27, 55
double-underline links, 10–11,
  23–26, 71–72
easy integration of, 13, 16
explaining to site visitors, 37,
  88, 90
good content and, 13–14, 16–17
hooks, 10, 28
hybrid in-text links, 67–68
icons and, 73–74
on image and video sites, 27
integrating with Google AdSense,
  75–77
link only, 64–65
lots of content and, 81
metrics and, 62, 63
mouse hover, 11
networks for, 38–42
noise balance, 60–61
nonintrusiveness of, 12, 15,
  60–61, 99
optimizing of, 15, 18
as pay-per-click (PPC) revenue,
  13, 16
penetration cycle and, 5–6, 93,
  98
as permission marketing, 14,
  17–18, 61–62, 98–99
placement of, 28
real estate and, 13–14, 17
related content in-text links,
  66–68
relevancy of, 14, 17, 61, 77–80
removal option for, 87–88,
  90–91

responding to complaints about,
87–93
returning users and, 89
as source of additional revenue,
13, 15–16
terminology, 10
terms to avoid, 29–30
text link ads and, 65–66
trial periods and, 39, 83–84
videos within, 63
iPad, 85–86
iPhones, 37, 84–85

K
Kindle, 86
Kontera, 38–39

L
Landing pages, 3, 30–33
Legal contracts, 83

M
Mac users, 34–35
MediaText, 40
Metrics, 62, 63
Mobile devices, 84–85
Mouse hover, 11
Multiple-level reporting, 81–82
MyGoodPage.com, 96–97

N
Net impressions, 44–45
Noise balance, 60–61

O
Online advertising

approval of in-text ads, 14, 18,
93–94
balance of risk and, 50–51
cycles of, 54–56
declining revenue of, 2–3
double-underline links and,
24–25
networks for, 38–42
niche content and, 82
penetration cycle, 4–6, 93, 98
seeking a wider audience, 52
tips to improve, 95–96
OnlineSiesta.com, 18, 101
Opera, 34

P
Payment threshold, 56–57, 59
Payments. *See* Revenue
Payoneer, 58
PayPal, 58, 59
Pay-per-acquisition (CPA), 16
Pay-per-click (PPC), 13, 16, 47–48,
51–52
Pay-per-lead (CPL), 16
Penetration cycle, 4–6, 93, 98
Permission marketing, vii, 6–7, 11,
14, 17–18, 61–62, 98–99
Permission Marketing (Godin), 6
Providers, 38–42

R
Related content in-text links, 66–68
Revenue
balance of risk and, 50–51
bottom-line, 46
business models and, 50
clicks and, 46–48
cycles in, 53–56
effective cost-per-mille (eCPM)
and, 43–44, 51, 55–56

floor PPC and, 51–52
formula for estimating, 48–50
international payments, 58
international traffic and, 45–46, 48
net impressions and, 44–45
payment methods, 57
payment threshold and, 56–57, 59
revenue share and, 52–53, 83
size of website and, 59
tax forms and, 58
transaction fees, 57
waiting period and, 56–57
See also Website monetization
Run-of-network (RON) campaigns, 70

S

Safari, 33–35
Search bubbles, 68–71
Shopping comparison bubbles, 70–71
Single-underline ad links, 72
Smart Context, 41
Snap, 66, 67
Spanish content, 86–87
Squidoo, 80, 81, 87, 93, 98, 99

T

Technology
automated processes and, 21, 55
dynamic ad placement, 20–21
IT infrastructure and, 22, 80
JavaScript code, 19–20
timing of the load, 20
Traffic arbitrage, 64, 70

V

Vibrant Media, 38–39, 41

W

Web browsers, 33–37
Website monetization
described, vii, 1
color of in-text links and, 26–27
double-underline format and, 23–26
large websites and, 59, 80–84
and opening in new window, 30–33
placement of hooks and, 28
terms to avoid, 29–30
web browsers and, 33–37
See also Revenue
Wikipedia, 66–67

Y

Yahoo Content Match, 8
YouTube, 66–67

Z

Zigzag underline format, 73